CU00760756

LADIES FIRST

The Story of Australia's First Olympic Hockey Gold Medal

LADIES FIRST

The Story of Australia's First Olympic Hockey Gold Medal

ASHLEY MORRISON

FAIRPLAY
PUBLISHING

First published in 2024 by Fair Play Publishing
PO Box 4101, Balgowlah Heights, NSW 2093, Australia
www.fairplaypublishing.com.au

ISBN: 978-1-923236-03-5

ISBN: 978-1-923236-04-2 (ePub)

© Ashley Morrison 2024

The moral rights of the author have been asserted.

All rights reserved. Except as permitted under the *Australian Copyright Act 1968* (for
example, a fair dealing for the purposes of study, research, criticism or review), no
part of this book may be reproduced, stored in a retrieval system, communicated or
transmitted in any form or by any means without prior written permission from the
Publisher.

Design and typesetting by Ismail Ogunbiyi.

Front cover photograph via Alamy. All other photographs
have been provided by the author, players, or Kevin Dempster.

All inquiries should be made to the Publisher via hello@fairplaypublishing.com.au

A catalogue record for this
book is available from the
National Library of Australia

I alone cannot change the world, but I can cast a stone across the water to create many ripples.

— **Mother Teresa**

CONTENTS

"MY HEROES"

I'm honoured to have been asked to write a tribute to this incredible team. Sadly, of the 16 women who played in Australia's first gold medal-winning hockey team, two have recently passed. Kathleen Partridge (who died in 2021) was the goalkeeper of that 1988 team that conquered all in Seoul, but she was also one of our coaches at the '96 Olympics in Atlanta, so I shared that connection with her. And Sandra Pisani (2022) was this fiercely strong half-back from South Australia, who I have fond memories of playing alongside in the Australian National Championships when I was 16. I was just in awe of the women in the Australian hockey team—Kathleen, Sandra and their teammates—who ultimately ignited a fire within me to want to one day follow in their footsteps.

In 1988, the team that ultimately won the gold in Seoul came to my hometown of Darwin for an acclimatisation camp en route to the Olympic Games. And it was where, because of me being on the junior pathway to the Australian national team, I got to play alongside members of that side. I could then, and can still now, throw a blanket over every single one of them and call them an inspiration for being such incredible women to people like me during that era. I became good friends with Elspeth Denning (Clement), who was selected for three Olympic Games and was later to become a valued mentor of mine throughout my journey to the Hockeyroos.

It was around that time that I realised many different people in your life can become an inspiration to you, and every single one of those women was.

For me, as this young kid from the Top End who had the lofty dreams of one day winning an Olympic gold medal, to know that I had trained with them, played alongside them, and then watched them go off to win Olympic gold was just phenomenal. It was an incredible time for me as this raw 17-year-old kid from the Top End, having the honour of watching those women achieve their ultimate goal. From then on, anything was possible!

While watching on television as the Hockeyroos won the Olympic final, I recall thinking how amazing it was that they were playing against South Korea in Korea. They weren't just facing a hockey team; they were playing against a whole nation cheering for the Australians to lose. Imagine how daunting it must have been to face an entire country!

As I watched them build a two-goal lead, I began to realise and focus anxiously on not only the result but the fact that two of our women had not played a single minute in the entire Olympic campaign—I could even sense the panic on the faces of the Australian players. You see, had Australia gone on to win gold—which they ultimately did—and had those two girls been left sitting on the bench when the final siren sounded, they would have missed out on standing atop the winning podium. The rules were clear: you had to have taken the field at some point in the campaign to be eligible to receive a medal on the podium. So, it was very nerve-racking to see whether the goal-keeping reserve, Maree Fish from Tasmania, and Lorraine Hillas, who went to the 1984 Olympics—both exceptional players in their own right—were going to take to the field before time ran out. The Hockeyroos' coach, Brian Glencross, had to swap his goalkeepers late in an Olympic final, plus find room for a defensive midfielder, and all that occurred in the last two minutes. Wow!

That was just one of many emotions surrounding that game. Had that not happened, I know it would have been a deflating moment for many of those girls. Yeah, you win Olympic gold, but two of your teammates would have missed out. And I think that is what makes team sports so great in terms of the camaraderie, the love and the friendship you share with your fellow teammates, because you're all on a journey and you're all after one common goal. It's the bond you all share in victory that molds you together and echoes for eternity.

Why have these great pioneers for women's sport been overlooked in the history books? When I won gold in 1996, it was the 100th year of the modern Olympiad, so attention around achievements that year seemed heightened. Like how Opening Ceremonies evolve from one Games to the next, so does the coverage of each Olympics, and perhaps our win in '96 came at a significant period of that evolution in coverage and recognition. There's no doubt the remarkable feats of that 1988 team have been cast in a shadow when compared with all those gold medal-winning teams that followed. Sadly, they haven't been honoured and celebrated enough.

1988 was the first time that any Australian hockey team had won an Olympic gold medal; the men's team, the Kookaburras, didn't win their first until 2004, by which time the women had won again in 1996 and 2000. The Hockeyroos had finished fifth in '92, then Ric Charlesworth took over and we won in '96 during what proved a golden decade for the sport in Australia. It seemed that every major tournament we entered from 1993 onwards was just gold, gold, gold. Then social media came along after the Sydney Games, where the hype for the present team was going north—and fast. There wasn't time for people to breathe and reflect and appreciate what those women achieved for the sport back in 1988; there was too much happening in the here and now. Well, that time has come. I know Ric Charlesworth appreciated that 1988 team: he had been there with the men's side in Seoul and often drew on the success of that women's team when coaching his other sides.

Make no mistake, that 1988 team was the foundation stone of Australian hockey at the Olympics. They proved winning gold was possible. Those mighty women who I idolised as a teenager are living legends of our sport. How important were they to my career? In 2023, long after I had retired as an athlete, then spent time in Federal Parliament and now have children and grandchildren chasing their own sporting dreams, I was honoured with induction into the Sport Australia Hall of Fame. There was only one person I wanted to drape the medal around my neck: Sharon Buchanan-Patmore. I chose Sharon because she was, and remains, one of my greatest heroes. Thank you, Sharon.

When I look at my gold medal from Atlanta, I smile when recalling how three of those girls from that legendary '88 team were on my team in 1996.

They played an enormous role in what we achieved that year. They brought knowledge, experience and composure to our thinking when they were able to say, "Okay, we're in an Olympic final, we've done it before, we know what we need to do." They were our leaders: Liane Tooth, Jackie Pereira and Rechelle Hawkes. They bound the two eras together, and it was a privilege to share both the hockey field and the winner's podium with those legends. Rechelle was also part of the 2000 triumph, she is a true legend of the sport.

I commend and congratulate Ashley Morrison on bringing the stories of that 1988 team—my heroes—out of the shadows for a modern audience to learn about. Because of his passion for the story of those mighty pioneering women, a new generation will now have the opportunity to celebrate a team that achieved remarkable things and who all deserve to be recognised and applauded.

Nova Peris OLY OAM
March 2024
Hockeyroos 1992–96
Olympic Gold: 1996 (Atlanta, USA)
Champions Trophy Gold: 1993 (Amstelveen, Netherlands), 1995 (Mar del Plata, Argentina)
World Cup Gold: 1994 (Dublin, Ireland)
Sports Hall of Fame—Hockeyroos 1996 Team, 2016

1. LADIES FIRST

An expression of courtesy indicating
that women should go first.

In days gone by, this saying was a part of Western etiquette. It was deemed correct behaviour to give ladies precedence over gentlemen.

Etiquette in those times did not prescribe that ladies should always pass first through a door or other narrow passage. In those times, a gentleman would only let a lady pass first when entering a trusted environment, such as his or her own home. If entering an unknown place, the man was expected to go first. The reason being that if any danger lurked on the other side of the door, the man could defend the 'poor defenceless damsel'.

History shows that many women went first and achieved feats in a male-dominated world.

When it comes to the sport of hockey in Australia, women have a habit of being ahead of men.

On July 2, 1910, the Australian Women's Hockey Association was formed and affiliated with the All-England Women's Hockey Association, which was the international governing body at the time. This was despite *Badminton* magazine describing the sport as "the most odious of all games for a woman".

No doubt looking to follow their lead, the men talked about forming an Australian Hockey Association as early as 1912. However, it would appear they talked about it for a very long time, as the Association did not come into existence until 1925. To be fair, there was the not-so-small matter of a World War from 1914-1918, which may well have played a major role in the delay.

The Australian women's team played their first international match on 1 August 1914 at Rushcutters Bay in Sydney and lost to England 11-3. Their next match, also against England, was in 1927; they lost 13-1 this time.

The men's first international game would be played eight years after the first women's match on 27 September 1922 in Palmerston North, New Zealand. They lost 5-4. By the time 1927 had come around they had played a further two matches against New Zealand and lost those as well.

The women's first international victory would come in their ninth international match in 1930. It came at the Empire Tournament in Southern Africa where they won 4-1 against Rhodesia.

The first international hat trick was scored by Mary Bloore (Bennett) from Victoria. She scored all four goals in a 4-1 victory over Belgium in Brussels on November 29, 1930. Eric Pearce scored the first hat trick from the men's team at the 1960 Rome Olympic Games against Japan.

The Olympic Games were steeped in male chauvinism for a very long time.

Baron Pierre de Coubertin, who is acknowledged as reviving the modern Olympic Games, certainly never saw women as equal partners. In his 'Ode to Sport', the centrality of the male athlete is clear. He never shied away from his view that women should not be included in the Olympic Games.

He gave three main reasons for his view. His first reason was an organisational one. He believed that problems would arise following the inclusion of women as there would be a need for the establishment of separate sports associations and the staging of separate events during the Olympic Games.

Second, he believed that it was inappropriate to view women competing in public sports competitions. His final reason was what he viewed as women's limited physical abilities, which made them "incapable of producing records in the highly competitive arena of the Olympic Games."

He said, "Can we allow women access to all Olympic events? No? Then why should some sports be open to them while the rest are not? Above all, what basis can one use to place the barrier between the events that are permitted, and those that are not? There are not just women tennis players and swimmers. There are women fencers, women riders and, in America, women rowers. Perhaps there will be women runners or even women football players in the future? Would such sports, played by women, constitute a sight to be recommended before the crowds that gather for an Olympiad? I do not think that any such claim can be made."

Oh, how wrong he was!

In those early days, the Games were reserved exclusively for the male athletes. At the 1900 Paris Olympic Games, Charlotte Cooper became the first female modern Olympic victor. She won the women's tennis singles gold medal. In Paris there were 997 athletes. Only 22 were women who competed in five sports: tennis, sailing, croquet, equestrianism and golf.

Four years later, the only event for women would be archery. The women who competed in these early Olympic Games tended to be from privileged backgrounds. They had the necessary funds and leisure time to enable their participation in what were deemed "acceptable sports".

The Baron did not shift from his viewpoint. In 1935, he said: "I personally do not approve of feminine participation in public competitions, which does not mean that women should not go in for a large number of sports, but I mean to say merely that they should not seek the limelight!"

Yet de Coubertin had a thorn in his side, a French woman called Alice Milliat.

In 1917 Alice Milliat helped form the Fédération Française Sportive Féminine, becoming treasurer and, in March 1919, its President.

In 1919, Milliat asked the International Association of Athletics Federations (IAAF) to include women's track and field athletics events in the 1924 Olympic Games, but they refused.

So Milliat went away and created the Fédération Sportive Féminine Internationale (FSFI). She initiated what became known later as the 1922 Women's World Games. Her aim was to ensure female control over women's international sporting competitions.

In August 1922, the Jeux Olympiques Féminins, regarded as the first

Women's Olympics, took place in Pershing Stadium in Paris. Five teams, representing the United States, Great Britain, Switzerland, Czechoslovakia and host country France competed. Eleven athletics events were conducted, and the 20,000-strong crowd saw eighteen athletes break world records. Milliat knew exactly what she was doing. She chose this venue because Paris was the home city of de Coubertin and she wanted the Games to be a showcase to the International Olympic Committee.

The Baron was President of the International Olympic Committee (IOC) from 1896–1925 and no doubt pleased to pass on the problem of Alice Milliat to his successor, Belgian Henri Comte de Baillet-Latour.

Milliat had intended her next Games to be hosted in Belgium, but with Baillet-Latour's election, Belgium changed their mind about hosting the event. This may well have been due to pressure coming directly from the new IOC President. The IOC were determined to quash Milliat. They eventually convinced her and the FSFI to change the name of their event in exchange for adding 10 women's events to the 1928 Olympics.

The next edition of her athletics event was held in Gothenburg, Sweden in 1926, and was now termed the Women's World Games. Due to constant pressure from the FSFI, the IOC eventually included five women's track and field events in the Amsterdam Olympics in 1928. Milliat was still not happy, because the men were allowed to compete in 22 events. She was not alone, and this lack of parity led to many women boycotting the Games.

Alice Milliat hosted her World Games again in 1930 and 1934. As the Berlin Olympic Games approached, she issued an ultimatum to the IAAF to fully integrate women's athletic events at the 1936 Olympics or cede all women's participation to the FSFI. An agreement was reached and the FSFI ceded control of international women's athletics to the IAAF in exchange for an expanded program. There was also one other condition—recognition of records set in the Women's Games.

While Alice Milliat launched the Women's World Games, the President of the All-England Women's Hockey Association in 1922, Mrs Heron Maxwell, put forward the idea of forming a body that would include all national women's sporting associations.

Two years later, following an international match between England and the USA, it was agreed to form such a body.

Around the same time, the International Olympic Committee had decided not to include hockey in the Paris Olympic Games. Frenchman Paul Leautey realised that the men's game needed an international body to promote the interests of the game globally and make sure it was included in the 1928 Olympic Games.

On 7 January 1924 following a meeting in Paris, it was decided to form the Federation Internationale de Hockey sur Gazon (FIH), and Leautey was elected the first President. The new body's role was to be responsible for technical issues, and to control the Olympic tournament. The opportunity to participate at the Olympic Games was a driving force in those early years for nations to become affiliated with the FIH.

While once again the women's game was ahead of their male counterparts, they took their time setting up the International Federation of Women's Hockey Associations (IFWHA). As there were several international sporting federations being created at the time, the women opted to compare the way they were structured and to adopt the best practices.

In 1927, an IFWHA constitution was submitted and accepted. The founding members were Australia, Denmark, England, Ireland, Scotland, South Africa, the USA and Wales. There was far more of a world feel about this body than the newly formed FIH, which was distinctly European. The founding member nations of the FIH were Austria, Belgium, Czechoslovakia, France, Hungary, Spain and Switzerland. Denmark joined in 1926, followed by Germany, India, Poland and Portugal in 1928.

In 1930, the USA women proposed that a tournament should be arranged to coincide with all future IFWHA conferences. This prompted the committee to set about developing rule uniformity.

It is interesting to note that the possibility of collaborating with the FIH was also discussed in 1930. These talks broke down over the definition of 'country'. The FIH ruled one country/one equal vote, and maintained that Great Britain was one country with Ireland separate. The IFWHA disagreed, feeling that an association with a large membership could be a greater asset than one with a small membership.

Further meetings were held in 1931 as the FIH set up a women's committee, but they broke down when the FIH refused to accept the IFWHA on an equal footing.

By 1948, most women's hockey associations were members of the IFWHA. As a result, an approach was made to the IOC for women's hockey to be included in the 1952 Olympic Games. The approach was rejected.

The hindsight of history now makes this decision more understandable. While the FIH would ensure hockey's Olympic inclusion in the 1928 Amsterdam Olympic Games, despite all of Alice Milliat's efforts and the Games welcoming more women's events, another chauvinist would take over as President of the IOC in 1952 – American Avery Brundage, better known to many as "Avery Umbrage".

He made his feelings about women participating quite clear. Prior to being elected President of the IOC, he held the position of Head of the Amateur Athletic Union, and in 1949 wrote: "I think it is quite well known that I am lukewarm on most of the [Olympic] events for women for a number of reasons which I will not bother to expound because I probably will be outvoted anyway. I think women's events should be confined to those appropriate for women: swimming, tennis, figure skating and fencing but certainly not shot putting."

In 1957, as President of the International Olympic Committee, he wrote to fellow members of the IOC in a letter: "Many still believe that events for women should be eliminated from the Games, but this group is now a minority. There is still, however, a well-grounded protest against events which are not truly feminine, like putting a shot, or those too strenuous for most of the opposite sex, such as distance runs."

However, rather than be dismayed by the rejection of the IOC in 1952, it only made the IFWHA more determined. They decided to focus their attention on their own tournaments and opted to move their triennial conference to a four-year cycle.

In 1959 with 15 teams attending the conference, the tournament had become a "World Cup" event. However, the IFWHA focus was very much on enjoyment and recreation. The aim was to keep the competitive spirit of teams under control, which was why their tournaments were not organised along championship lines.

Three years earlier in 1956, Australia's men's hockey team had competed at the Olympic Games for the first time when Melbourne was the host city.

Despite the ladies having been first in so many areas of the game, there was nothing that they could do when it came to Olympic participation. The sport would still have a very long wait before it was welcomed into the Olympic family.

The first time women appeared at the Olympic Games in a hockey tournament was in 1980. It was agreed that this event would be organised by the IFWHA, however after the Games they would join the FIH This merger was finalised in 1983.

Australia's women would make their first Olympic appearance on the hockey field at the 1984 Games in Los Angeles.

From 1922 to the start of 1956 when the Australian men made their Olympic debut as the host nation in Melbourne, they had played 14 international matches – 13 against New Zealand and one against India. By comparison up until the start of 1956, the women's team had played 41 international matches against 14 countries.

The word lady and the term 'ladies first' are seen as old-fashioned today, which is a great shame. Both are a sign of respect.

While many of the 1988 gold medal-winning side have laughed at being labelled 'ladies', it is the correct term. As a group, they deserve our respect. They were the first Australian team to win an Olympic gold medal.

The team that represented Australia at the 1988 Olympic Games was as follows:

Tracey Belbin
Deborah Bowman-Sullivan
Sharon Buchanan (Patmore)
Lee Capes
Michelle Capes

Sally Carbon

Elspeth Denning (Clement)

Loretta Dorman

Maree Fish

Rechelle Hawkes

Lorraine Hillas

Kathleen Partridge

Jacqueline Pereira

Sandra Pisani

Kim Small

Liane Tooth

Coach: Brian Glencross

Assistant Coach: Peter Freitag

Team Manager: Yvonne Parsons

Doctor: Tony Galvin

Team Psychologist: Brian Miller

N.B.: There was much debate as to which names to use for certain players as some have changed their names since the 1988 Olympic Games. After discussions with the individuals concerned, it was decided to go with the names that they are best known by.

2. LEADING UP TO SEOUL

"I want to make Seoul the front line of the new South Korea. Seoul is sleeping, and I want to wake it up."

South Korean politician Chung Mong-joon

On 30 September 1981 at the 11th Olympic Congress in Baden-Baden, West Germany, Seoul was awarded the rights to host the 1988 Summer Olympic Games.

It had been decided that the Olympic Games would head to Asia for the second time, and the final vote was between Nagoya in Japan and Seoul in South Korea. Seoul was the favourite going into Congress as Japan had been the only Asian nation to host the Olympic Games in Tokyo in 1964.

The vote reflected that favouritism, with Seoul winning 52 votes to 27.

The timing of the announcement was important for the country as on 26 October 1979, the nation's third President Park Chung Hee had been assassinated.

His death ended the Bu-Ma Democratic Protests. On 16 October that year, students from Pusan National University began demonstrations calling for the abolition of Park Chung Hee's Yushin regime.

Park had come to power as the head of a military dictatorship following the May 16 military coup d'état in 1961. His election brought about the start of the Third Republic in 1963. He and his government created a series of economic policies that brought rapid economic growth and industrialisation to the nation. This became known as the 'Miracle on the Han River'. In the 1960s and 1970s, South Korea possessed one of the fastest-growing national economies.

At the end of the 1970s, that growth began to slow and, as a result, Park's popularity started to wane. The 1971 Presidential election proved much closer than expected. However, Park prevailed and remained in office.

In 1972, Park declared martial law and amended the constitution into a highly authoritarian document called the 'Yushin Constitution'. The pretence was that the Yushin Constitution was the seventh constitutional amendment. However, it actually abolished South Korea's former constitution.

Martial law was declared across the country, and work began on the new constitution. It was said that Park had drawn inspiration for his coup from Ferdinand Marcos, the then President of the Philippines, who had orchestrated a similar coup just a few weeks earlier.

The Yushin Constitution was an extremely authoritarian document. It gave the President sweeping executive and legislative powers and extended his term in office to six years with no limit on re-election.

The President also had the right to appoint one-third of the National Assembly, which effectively guaranteed him a parliamentary majority. The Yushin Constitution basically codified Park's emergency powers since December and turned his presidency into a legal dictatorship.

Understandably, there were protests, but political opposition and dissent were constantly repressed. To help his cause, Park had complete control of the media and military.

In 1979, the student protests gained momentum and started to spread. President Park Chung Hee declared martial law on 18 October, and 66 people were referred to the Military Court. Two days later, Park invoked the Garrison Act. He mobilised the army, and 59 civilians were brought before the Military Court.

Less than a week later, Park, four bodyguards and his chauffeur were killed in a safe house by the Head of the Korean Central Intelligence Agency.

After 18 years of dictatorship, the country immediately went into turmoil, and stability did not return for a year.

In August 1980, Chun Doo-hwan was elected President. He was unopposed and, not surprisingly, won 99.4% of the vote.

In October of that year, Chun abolished all political parties and established his own, the Democratic Justice Party. This was effectively a rebranding of Park's Democratic Republican Party, which had ruled South Korea since 1963. Chun also enacted a new constitution that was less authoritarian than Park's Yushin Constitution. However, it still gave the President broad powers.

He dissolved the Fourth Republic in March 1981 when he was formally inaugurated as President after being re-elected in the February 1981 election.

Like so many political leaders before and since, Chun saw sport as an important tool in achieving positive outcomes for his government. He submitted South Korea's bid to host the 1988 Olympics to the IOC in September 1981. He did so in the hope that the increased international exposure brought by hosting the Olympic Games would legitimise his authoritarian regime. Chun hoped it would also reduce the increasing political pressure for democratisation in South Korea and provide protection from increasing threats from North Korea. The Games would also help to showcase the Korean economic miracle to the world.

South Korea became the first mainland Asian nation to win hosting rights for the Olympic Games. The Games would eventually give the South Koreans new opportunities to forge new economic relationships and grow their international trade.

The International Olympic Committee did face a problem after announcing Seoul as the host city – the distinct lack of diplomatic relations between South Korea and the then-communist countries.

The IOC witnessed a boycott by communist countries at the Los Angeles Games in 1984 and was desperate to avoid a similar occurrence in 1988. Having such a boycott at two Olympic Games in a row would damage their integrity.

At one stage, the IOC did consider taking the Games back to Munich instead of Seoul, but eventually, the communist countries agreed to participate in Seoul.

One development because of this uncertainty was that the IOC decided to send the invitations to the 1988 Games rather than leaving that task to the Games organising committee, as had been the case in the past.

However, there would still be another problem for the IOC – Cuban President Fidel Castro had suggested that North Korea should be a joint host of the Games.

Then IOC President Juan Antonio Samaranch chaired a meeting of the North and South Korean Olympic Committees on 8 and 9 January 1986 in Lausanne, Switzerland. At this meeting, North Korea tabled its hosting demands. They wanted 11 of the 23 Olympic sports to be held in North Korea and demanded special Opening and Closing Ceremonies. In addition, North Korea wanted a joint organising committee and a united Korean team. To their credit, the IOC and South Korea did not dismiss these demands immediately. Negotiations continued into a second meeting, where they collapsed.

The fallout was that North Korea, Cuba, Albania and Ethiopia opted to boycott the event.

Nicaragua withdrew as well, but this was mainly due to financial considerations. Madagascar was expected to compete, but also withdrew due to financial reasons just before the Opening Ceremony. As for the Seychelles, they simply did not reply to the invitation to attend.

While the various nations bidding to host the 1988 Olympic Games were gearing up for the 1981 hosting announcement, a great deal had been happening in Australia.

Winning medals became more important than ever during the Cold War and specifically since 1956, when Melbourne hosted the Olympic Games.

It is believed that the Russians erected a medal table in the Olympic Village in Melbourne, and they were determined to score propaganda points by winning more medals than their archrival, the USA. By creating a medal table, not only would it symbolise superiority, but it would also rub the United States' noses in it.

When the Melbourne Games wrapped up, Russia topped the medal tally with 98 – 37 gold, 29 silver, and 32 bronze. The USA was second with 74 medals—32 gold, 25 silver, and 17 bronze.

Hosts Australia came third with a total of 35 medals.

The Soviet Union would top the medal tally again in 1960 in Rome. In Tokyo in 1964, a new way of judging a nation's success was used. Suddenly, the number of gold medals won would take precedence over the overall total number of medals won. Was this a case of political manoeuvring behind the scenes? It enabled the USA to reclaim top spot with 36 gold medals to the Soviet Union's 30, even though the Soviet Union won more medals overall—96 to the USA's 90.

The USA deservedly topped the tally in Mexico in 1968, and maybe that humiliation led to the now-known drug enhancement program in the Soviet Union in the 1970s. The Soviet Union claimed the top spot again in 1972 and 1976, while East Germany climbed above the USA, which finished third.

The 1976 Olympic Games in Montreal would be a turning point for Australian sport. Australia finished 32nd on the medal tally winning four bronze medals – two in sailing, one in swimming and one in equestrian. The Australian Olympic team did not win a single gold medal. A solitary silver medal came in hockey where the men lost the gold-medal match to New Zealand.

There was a sense of shame back in Australia. This was the worst Olympic performance since the 1936 Games where the nation had managed a solitary bronze medal, won by Jack Metcalfe in the triple jump.

The federal government was quick to realise how the sporting performances of a nation can impact its mood and have an affect at the ballot box. It also impacted how the country was perceived overseas.

Prime Minister Malcolm Fraser set about creating an elite sports training program in Australia, ironically modelled on the East German system. The Hon. Robert Ellicott, the Minister for Home Affairs and the Environment, announced the establishment of the Australian Institute of Sport (AIS) on 25 January 1980. Prime Minister Fraser officially opened the AIS exactly one year and one day later on Australia Day in 1981.

The first sports into the AIS program were basketball, gymnastics, netball, swimming, tennis, track and field, football and weightlifting.

Prior to the opening of the AIS, there was a major development for hockey.

A federal government announcement came in 1978 that funding would be made available to build a hockey stadium of international standard in Perth to coincide with Western Australia's 150-year anniversary in 1979. It would include a water-based pitch and other support facilities. It became the first water-based pitch in the Southern Hemisphere at the time.

Once built, the Commonwealth Hockey Stadium (as it was known then) was opened by Prime Minister Malcolm Fraser. It hosted the Esanda International tournament as its first event. Crowds were so big that the gates had to be locked twice.

In 1984, hockey was added to the elite sports training program being run by the AIS. It became the first sport to be based outside of Canberra, being located in Perth, Western Australia. This was a decision that is still debated over four decades later.

The two men that headed up the initial AIS hockey program were the two national coaches at the time. Richard Aggiss, who was the coach of the men, and Brian Glencross who had been appointed women's coach in 1980. They had started work on setting up the program the year before.

Brian came from a hockey family. Some would say it was his destiny. His father, Ron, was well known in hockey circles as he wrote the hockey articles for the *Sunday Times* newspaper during the 1960s and 1970s. Brian and his older brothers, Ron and Denis, all played hockey at the YMCA club. All three represented Western Australia. Denis was selected for Australia in 1965 while Brian earned his first cap a year earlier.

The boys' younger sister, Ros, played for the Surf Hockey club. It is important to note that at the time, the men's and women's clubs were separate, as was the administration of the game.

Brian started his hockey at Kent Street High School and came through the junior ranks at YMCA, making his First Division debut in 1959. He played for YMCA for the next 20 years and had one season with Fremantle in 1980.

He was first selected for Western Australia in 1961 and played his last match for WA in 1977. His first national selection came in 1964 when he was a part of the squad competing at the Tokyo Olympics.

His was a surprise selection by coach Charlie Morley, and no one was more surprised than Glencross himself. "We played the National Championships in Perth, Western Australia didn't win it, but that night they selected the team for '64. It was the first time I had been in the team; it was a joyous time. It was a Saturday night; I can remember the day. One of the things at that time was we had a very close-knit WA team and quite a lot of national team players in those days, because WA were quite strong in Hockey, and some of the people I thought should have got in didn't get in, so there was a bit of a mixture joy and excitement for some and disappointment for others. Although for me, the joy part was a lot stronger than the disappointment," he admitted.

This was a time when there were no rolling substitutions, so Brian had to bide his time. He was eventually given his chance and kept his place in the team as Australia went on to win their first Olympic medal for hockey – a bronze by beating Spain 3-2 after extra time. Don McWatters scored the equaliser to take the game into extra time before Eric Pearce scored his second and Australia's third.

Brian was also a part of the team four years later in Mexico. This time Australia progressed all the way to the gold-medal match where they met Pakistan.

"It was a pretty tough match because there had been a few incidents with Pakistan during the round games, sticks flying and people being hit, and stuff like that," he recalled. "In the final, I was acting captain because Don McWatters who was captain never played a game because of his back injury, and I remember shouting this to the players because they were about to bop a Pakistani – I said, 'let's win it'. [It was important] Not to get carried away because the tension was so great."

Pakistan took the lead through Abdul Rashid, but it was Brian who equalised for Australia.

Then came a moment that he would remember and replay the rest of his life. "We were so close, yet in some situations, so far away playing against Pakistan. We lost that final 2-1. I remember I scored, but I also remember the other one that I got that they blew up because it was handled. In the old days they used to hand-stop, and it was supposed to be stopped dead. Well, the umpire, I am not sure what country he came from, said it moved." He chuckled as he replayed the moment in his mind "It went in the goals, and that would have put us in front. So that was how close that game was. I used to replay that one in my mind a lot, you know, what if?"

So, Brian had to settle for Australia's first Olympic silver hockey medal to go with their first bronze from four years earlier. He went on to play at the Munich Olympic Games in 1972, but Australia finished outside of the medals in fifth place.

He summed up that result by simply saying: "In '72, we didn't have the team we had in '68. There was a big changeover, so therefore we weren't as good a team as we were as individuals."

He played his last game for Australia in 1974 and finished his international career having played 93 games for Australia. It is worth remembering that in his era, teams did not play as much international hockey. He attended three Olympic Games and was captain of the side at two of them.

Like many players, he moved into coaching and when given the reins of the Australian women's national team in 1980, he was just the second male to be made their coach. Merv Adams had taken on the role in 1979.

As a coach, it has been said that he was hard. He expected those around him to put in the required effort, and he had little time for those he felt were not trying their hardest. Another attribute that he had was being incredibly well organised.

With the Australian Institute of Sport opening in Perth, many of the top players from the east coast of Australia were invited to head across to Western Australia.

Liane Tooth was one of those invited from New South Wales. "They'd never had a hockey program like that in Australia, so I think it was a bit of a learning experience for everyone, the players, and the coaches, to learn how to manage a program," she recalled. "Like your body getting used to training so much compared to how little we probably trained in comparison to what they do now. I think from memory several of us got a few overuse injuries at the start of it, because our bodies weren't used to it. I think the coaching staff and all of us kind of learnt along the way to get to a balanced program. We learnt how many really intense sessions you could do and how to balance that against strength and conditioning, along with some development sessions where the focus was on the skill and not on the intensity. I think we were really starting to reap the benefits of that by the time the Seoul Olympics came along because the program had been going for four years by then. So, there'd been a significant improvement in all of us by then because we were suddenly training a lot more, both as a team and a squad and individually working on our own individual skills."

Many of the young men and women who came across to Western Australia to join the hockey program were housed in the Noalimba Hostel. It had been built in 1968 as a migrant hostel to house the 'ten-pound poms' and other migrants who opted to call Australia home.

This meant that the Noalimba Hostel was empty, so it became the perfect lodging for the hockey program. Noalimba was demolished in 2003 and replaced by new housing and a park, but for many who stayed there, it holds some very special memories.

"Everyone had to do Noalimba. If you hadn't done Noalimba, you hadn't done the AIS!" Debbie Bowman said with a laugh.

"I was very fortunate that my partner from the Gold Coast, who I ended up marrying, came across too, and I was able to move out of Noalimba and into a unit with him in Victoria Park."

"It was interesting in the fact that it was a migrant hostel, and you came back from training, and we were all worried about our weight back then, and the fish was just sitting in butter. There was Brian telling us to watch our weight, and we would come home and look at the food and think, that is just not edible. There was also the security side of it; if someone left the door open, it opened to all our inner doors, the guys were downstairs, and we were upstairs."

"We had the AIS minibus that we were responsible for, and there were many tales of the bus driving through bottle shop drive-thrus, and we got told off because you shouldn't be taking an AIS bus through a drive-thru," Debbie recalled with a nostalgic chuckle.

"The most daunting side for me was losing my hairdressing job in Queensland and going over to Perth, as that was my security. It wasn't so much family-based, more that it was hard to get a job back then. I was working for Stefan Hair Fashions in Queensland, which was quite big. He did have a sister shop in Perth, and he was able to get me a job there in the middle of Perth in one of the malls. However, it was totally different hairdressing. I was doing mainly family hairdressing in Queensland, but working at First Knot, it was all punk haircuts incorporating all sorts of colours, and I thought maybe not my style."

"So, I needed another job, and I pulled chickens apart for a day in a takeaway. That wasn't for me either. Then in Mount Hawthorn, there was a lovely lady who had a salon where she worked by herself, and she said you can come and work with me and do your hours in the middle of the day and do your training in the morning and at night, and we became long-term friends."

"I came from New South Wales, so yes, I moved into Noalimba," Liane Tooth explained. "That was an interesting experience. It was fun but challenging on occasions, but it was all part of the experience. I think we became a really good, fun bunch of people who became good friends, and living in the same vicinity as the men in their program as well, that was a new experience for everyone. But most of the Western Australians were, I think, allowed to live at home. There were a couple that moved in there, Jackie Pereira and Michelle Capes, if I remember correctly."

Liane's memory was spot on, as Michelle verified. "It was funny because it was only me, Jackie, Loretta [Dorman], Kathy [Partridge], Liane and the rest of the other girls from the eastern States who weren't in the Olympic team. Kim Small and all the older girls, like Lee [Capes], Lorraine [Hillas] and Sandy Pisani, they all lived at home."

"They were great times. Loretta Dorman, who was a very churchy person, never swore, never drank; Jackie and I said to her at the beginning of the year, 'By the end of the year we're going to have you drinking, swearing and partying', and she's like, 'no'. She used to go to the church when she first arrived at the AIS. By the end of the year, we changed her. Jackie used to go home for a Sunday roast every week without fail for the first couple of months, and then she stopped. After that, we were too busy partying or going out or doing something we shouldn't have been doing," Michelle recalled with a laugh before adding thoughtfully, "Yeah, they were the best two years."

Loretta had a similar view of Noalimba as Liane. "I think the best part about it was everyone was in the same boat, so it was almost like, 'right, one in all in'. We had each other to keep ourselves going. It definitely wasn't ideal. You were in a room where the door opened, and you were on an outdoor balcony. We walked down to get food, and it wasn't home-cooked food, it was like you were on a camp. We had the guys living there too, and most of the guys hadn't lived out of home, so I still remember some of the girls taking them down to show them how to do the washing! You know, just those funny memories, we had some fantastic times there. It was ideal because we were all in it together and the whole thing was new, like the Institute, and the training. It wasn't the best accommodation, but it was good fun."

Sharon Buchanan was another person who lived in Noalimba, and she remembered their daily schedule.

"We would get up at 5.30am, go to training, have a quick breakfast and a shower and then a lot of the girls would go off to work. Then we'd be back at training at 4.30-5.00pm. Sometimes after that, we would be in the gym, or we would go to club training. Then the next day, we would do it all over again."

"I think Friday we had off. Sundays, we would do a 10 km run around the river. We were busy, and we didn't have the money to enable us not to work. It wasn't an option to not work for most of us," she explained.

"Once a week, we trained with the local clubs and played for them at the weekend. I loved my club hockey. It gives you a chance to play freely and try things that you want to do. It was a little more relaxed, which was why it was fun."

"It must have been hard in those days to move from the east to the west," Elspeth Denning sympathised but felt that this was the making of the team. "From '84, most of us were still playing, and we were a pretty close group, and remember there were seven girls from WA, so we were close, and the Institute of Sport was here, so everyone was together. I think that really helped having everyone here in one central place because we were all close. However, it was hard as we got nothing for training. We had to train early in the morning, work, and then come to training after work, and then we also trained on weekends. So, you had to be committed."

Unfortunately, Australia did not send a team to the 1980 Moscow Olympic Games hockey tournament. If ever there was a time where politics crossed the line into sport, this was it.

The Moscow Olympics were the first ever appearance of women's hockey at the Olympic Games, but a boycott due to the Soviet Union's invasion of Afghanistan saw many of the major hockey- playing nations not participate. Only 80 of 147 nations competed.

While many nations boycotted en masse, Australia was in a different situation. The Australian government did not "encourage" participation, and those from Australia who did compete were not allowed to carry the national flag.

The Australian teams to attend the Olympic Games and participate in the hockey tournament were announced, and those selected for the first ever women's Olympic team were:

Marian Aylmore (WA)

Sharon Buchanan (WA)

Elspeth Denning (WA)

Di Troode (WA)

Janice Davidson WA)

Pamela Glossop (QLD) – Vice-Captain

Diane Gorman (NSW) – Captain

Julene Grant (Qld)

Sandra Grant (NSW)

Kym Ireland (QLD)

Robyn Leggatt (NSW)

Robyn Morrison (QLD)

Colleen Pearce (WA)

Jan Ramshaw (WA)

Sharyn Simpson (QLD)

Susan Skirrow (WA)

Elspeth Denning's had been a very different journey to international honours.

Her father had played hockey and rugby union for Kenya and East Africa. Elspeth was born in Kenya and was one of six children – three girls and three boys. All proved to be good at sports. Her sister Louise played State hockey in Western Australia and her brothers were all good rugby players and surfers.

When Elspeth was seven, the family moved from Kenya to South Africa where they lived in Cape Town until she was 19. Then they moved to Australia.

"We came in 1976 and I was selected to play for Australia in 1979, but I didn't think I had an Australian passport, so they whipped it through fast. Now it is law that you must have that country's passport, but back then it was not so strict," she admitted.

"I was picked for the 1980 Games. It was really annoying for us as we were asked if we wanted to go. We said, 'yes' and then they said, 'well we will make the decision'. The next thing we know they said, 'no one is going', and then other sports went, and we thought 'what the hell?'" The frustration is still as fresh as if it were yesterday.

The Australian Olympic Commission (AOC) voted on whether they should send a team. It was a close-run thing with the vote going 6/5 in favour of defying the government of the day's wishes and sending a team to the Olympic Games. However, ultimately it came down to the individual sports.

Prime Minister Malcolm Fraser was very vocal in his support of the request to boycott the Games by the United States President, Jimmy Carter. Immense political pressure was applied to some individual sports.

Only in recent times has it been made clear that threats to funding of certain sports were made, and inducements by way of compensation for not attending were offered.

The announcement that hockey would be going came on a Friday evening, but by early the next week that decision had been overturned. Hockey along with yachting, shooting equestrian and volleyball all decided not to send teams.

Even though the men's and women's hockey programs were run separately, there were close ties.

The Australian Hockey Association had very close ties to the Prime Minister's office. Frank Yeend was Vice-President of the Australian Hockey

Association. His brother Geoffrey was the Prime Minister's private secretary. The board of the Australian Hockey Association, which ran the men's game, voted not to send a team. The women were not bound by that decision, but it would have been hard to go when the men announced a day later that they would join the boycott.

Sharon Buchanan was chosen to represent the national team following the National Championships in Hobart at the end of '79 and picked for the Olympic squad in 1980.

"I was in the squad at 16 and the Olympic squad at 17," she explained. "It was tragic we did not go, particularly for those players who were never to play again. They had to retire. I was fortunate that I was at the start of my career, and I had other opportunities."

Di Troode, Janice Davidson, Diane Gorman, Sandra Grant, Robyn Morrison, Jan Ramshaw, Sharyn Simpson and Susan Skirrow would never be given the opportunity to fulfil their Olympic dream. It was cruelly taken away from them.

Half of the squad – eight players who had been selected for the Olympic Games in Moscow and issued with their uniforms – would never be given the opportunity to step onto a pitch and officially able to call themselves Olympians. Australian officials assured them that they would always be regarded as Olympic athletes, but the International Olympic Committee took a different view.

Even in Australia it appears that the promise made was a hollow one as these athletes are sadly still not recognised as Olympic athletes by the Australian Olympic Committee today, or by their own sport.

"We were chosen to go to the Olympics and given certificates saying we were Olympians and also given the blazers, but in the eyes of the world, we weren't because we never went, we never played a game," Elspeth confirms.

Sharon Buchanan echoed those thoughts, speaking with genuine sadness in her voice even after all these years. "I think the sad thing was that that team wasn't recognised. I mean we got a uniform and everything, but it is still not recognised. The team was named, and it is sad that some of those players were never recognised for being in the team."

"What was annoying was [that] Australia supposedly boycotted the Games, but they didn't really! Some people would never go to another Games, they were robbed of that opportunity," Elspeth states with passion. "I was lucky I was young and at the beginning of my career, but it still worried me even though I knew I would have another chance. But I felt it was so unfair on so many of the other girls who never had a chance to go to another Olympics. For some, that was the end of their career."

In Moscow, only six teams contested the women's hockey. The format was a round robin with the top team claiming gold. Zimbabwe, with three wins and two draws, was the only undefeated side and took home the gold. Czechoslovakia took silver and the Soviet Union bronze.

The Zimbabwe women became the first women's team to win Olympic gold. As the story goes, it was announced on their return home that their reward for their success was an ox each, although none of them ever received one.

Despite the disappointment of not participating at the Moscow Games, Brian Glencross had a job to do. He had to pick the team up from that disappointment and prepare them for the team's first appearance at a Women's Hockey World Cup since the women were now under the control of the International Hockey Federation.

Following a tour of the United States in October 1980 where the team was unbeaten, hopes were high for a podium finish.

The World Cup was held in Buenos Aires and Australia started well with a 6-0 win over Austria. They dropped one game in their pool to the Netherlands and finished second, which meant that they were through to the semi-finals.

Unfortunately, they suffered a 2-1 semi-final loss to West Germany. This meant that they would play-off for bronze against Russia, who backed up their Olympic bronze medal with a 5-1 victory. Australia had to settle for fourth.

In the next three years leading up to the 1984 Los Angeles Olympic Games, and including the 1983 World Cup, the team would play 40 games, winning 17, drawing 11 and losing 12.

At the 1983 World Cup, the team claimed the bronze medal thanks to two goals from Elspeth Denning and one from Julene Grant in securing a 3-1 victory over West Germany. The Germans solitary goal came from Martina Koch.

There was reason to be optimistic for their debut appearance at the Olympic Games in Los Angeles. The team selected was:

Marian Aylmore (WA)
Evelyn Botfield (VIC)
Sharon Buchanan (WA)
Elspeth Denning (WA)
Loretta Dorman (ACT)
Penelope Dunbabin (TAS)
Pamela Glossop (QLD)
Julene Grant (QLD)
Tricia Heberle (WA)
Lorraine Hillas (QLD)
Robyn Holmes (QLD)
Kym Ireland (QLD)
Robyn Leggatt (NSW)
Colleen Pearce (WA)
Sandra Pisani (SA)
Liane Tooth (NSW) – replacement
Susan Carlson-Jones (SA)

Prior to heading to Los Angeles, Australia had gone to Germany and London for some warm-up games against West Germany and England. In the second of these games against Germany at Bad Durkheim, which finished 3-3, Elspeth Denning was among the scorers but she injured her thumb.

"I was upset when I missed Moscow, but I wasn't devastated," Elspeth recalled. "I was more upset in '84 when I was there, and I shattered my hand against Germany and I couldn't play. Brian was saying 'you have to keep going', but I was saying, 'I am not sure I can keep doing this'. Liane (Tooth) stepped in. They flew her over a couple of days before the tournament started."

As they say, one person's misfortune is another's gain, and that is never truer than in sport. For Liane Tooth it was far from easy coming in and replacing Elspeth as she explained.

"Oh, it was incredibly difficult, you know, her disappointment obviously and being injured so close to the Olympics. I wasn't an established member of the team or anything, so I didn't know the girls that well. I knew some of them because they were obviously training in Perth in the lead-up to get themselves ready. I guess back then it was kind of a little bit more the team and the substitutes. So, the team would be practising stuff and there were a few of us that were definitely more likely to be 'benchies' that would tend to get some other stuff to do. Not all the time, but sometimes. So, it was certainly challenging, but I don't feel like I was treated like an outsider by any of the girls. I did know them, but it was a difficult situation because they were all obviously disappointed for Elspeth as well, and Elspeth couldn't come into the village, but she was still over there, so it was hard."

"I met the team in Vancouver, not long before they were due to move into the Olympic Village," Liane remembered. "So, that was where I played my first official game for Australia. I only played a few minutes in one game of the '84 Olympics, it was against New Zealand, and I think we were maybe 3-0 up by then. The rules were different back then. That's when we only had two substitutes. So, I guess the coaching was a lot more conservative in terms of making changes, particularly defenders. So, I spent a lot of the first couple of years on the bench learning and watching."

For Elspeth, it was even worse. "I stayed on and watched the tournament, but if I was given the choice again, I would come home. It was awful sitting there in the stands, particularly on the last day when we lost everything. All I could do was sit and cry with them."

As with Moscow four years earlier, the women's Olympic competition would be contested between six teams and every team would play each other. The team finishing top of the table would win the gold medal.

Australia's first Olympic outing was on 1 August 1984 at the Weingart Stadium at East Los Angeles College in Monterey Park, California. The stadium was built in 1951 at a cost of $3.1 million, and after being especially renovated in 1984, it was renamed after philanthropist Ben Weingart.

Weingart was a self-made man and became one of the richest men in California, building a fortune of nearly $100 million. The Weingart Foundation, his philanthropic organisation, provided grants and support to many charitable causes. It is said to have granted more than $950 million in support of various Southern Californian social services, including educational and community programs.

The first game was against West Germany who were no doubt looking to avenge their World Cup bronze medal loss and climb back to the top, having won two World Cups prior to that defeat. This too was their first Olympic appearance.

Australia found themselves 2-0 down, with Martina Koch opening the scoring in the 22nd minute and three minutes later, Corinna Lingnau doubled West Germany's lead. That was how the score remained until halftime.

Australia fought back in the second half and Sharon Buchanan scored Australia's first women's Olympic goal seven minutes after the break. Then Sandy Pisani scored with one minute left on the clock to tie things up, and the game finished a draw.

Next up the following day were trans-Tasman rivals New Zealand. Thanks to goals from Buchanan, Trish Heberle and Kym Ireland, Australia recorded a 3-0 victory.

For both teams, this was their second match. New Zealand had now lost both. Australia's win saw them move to the top of the table on three points; there were only two points awarded for a win at the time.

The following day the Netherlands won again, and so reclaimed top spot with a maximum four points. West Germany also won and joined Australia on three. The matches for these two teams against the Netherlands were shaping up as being the ones to decide the medals.

On 4 August, the USA recorded its second victory, so suddenly they too were in the mix.

The following day the Netherlands defeated West Germany 6-2 in the morning game. Australia met Canada late in the afternoon knowing that a victory would lift them into second place. But it wasn't to be.

Canada took the lead in the 10th minute through Laura Branchaud. Susan

Watkins levelled the scores in the 25th minute, and that is how it remained until the 54th minute when Sheila Forshaw slotted home to claim victory for Canada.

This meant that the Netherlands were now in pole position with a maximum six points from three games, the USA were on four with West Germany and Australia on three.

West Germany defeated New Zealand the next day. Canada held the Netherlands to a 2-2 draw and Australia recorded a much-needed 3-1 victory over the USA thanks to a double from Trish Heberle from penalty corners, and a field goal from Julene Grant.

On 9 August, West Germany and the USA played out a 1-1 draw.

The result meant that heading into their final match against the Netherlands, Australia knew that a win would lift them level on points with their opponents. A draw would see them level with West Germany in second spot. Australia was unlikely to match the Netherlands' superior goal difference, but a victory would see them have a better goal difference than West Germany, and thus claim the silver medal.

However, all these calculations became irrelevant when the Netherlands were victorious, 2-0. Australia was still in the match until the second goal was scored with three minutes to go. The victory secured the gold medal for the Dutch and assured West Germany of silver. But there was a problem when it came to the bronze medal.

Both Australia and the USA had finished on five points along with Canada. Both had won two games, drawn one and lost two. Both teams had scored nine goals, and both had conceded seven, so their goal difference was identical.

In many competitions today when this occurs, the way to separate the two teams is to go back to the result when they played each other. If that had been the case, Australia would have claimed the bronze medal following their 3-1 victory. However, that was not how things were done back in 1984.

Having had the gold medal within their grasp, the players had seen that slip from view. They had also witnessed their claim to outright bronze being snatched from them with three minutes left in their final match. The Australians were then told that the medal would be decided in a penalty shoot-out. This would take place just 15 minutes after the end of their match against the Netherlands.

The USA players had not had a game on that final day and so had to get changed and participate in the shoot-out decider. Ten outfield players from each side were required to beat the opposing goalkeeper from the penalty spot.

Australia immediately was at a disadvantage after missing their opening two attempts. At 4-2, the USA was yet to miss, and when Australia missed the next two attempts to make it 6-2, it was all but over. The final score was 10-5 to the USA who did not miss a single attempt.

Under the cruellest of circumstances, Australia had now seen the bronze medal slip from their grasp.

"I don't think I felt the disappointment as hard as the girls that had been in that team for a lot longer than I had, and I probably didn't fully appreciate that it wasn't really fair for them to have just played a game, and essentially lost two medals. To go through that disappointment and then having just played a full-on game of hockey while the USA are out the back practising their strokes and having not played. They were very fresh. It wasn't a fair way to decide the outcome," was Liane Tooth's memory of that day.

"The USA team were there out the back of the ground practising their penalty strokes as they did not have a game that day, while we played the toughest team in the competition, the Dutch. At the end of our game, we had to go and take strokes in a penalty shoot-out. So, we ended up in fourth place, and not surprisingly everyone was a little despondent," Lorraine Hillas remembered. "To be honest, I think we played some pretty good hockey and could be proud of how we played. There were some highlights. There were some fabulous athletes in that team. It was sad, but it was what it was."

Despite coming so close to a medal, there was little fanfare for the women's team. Women's sport in the 1980's still struggled to gain any media airtime.

Benjamin Franklin famously said, 'out of adversity comes opportunity'. Sharon Buchanan is convinced that from the hurt of that day came a determination and a realisation that this team could achieve greatness.

"It was a very different situation back then," she explained. "1984 was the first time that the Australian women had been in the Olympic Games, and we were being coached by Brian, who had a very strong emotional connection to the men; I'm sure he would have said the same thing. So, in '84 it was still very much all about the men, and our performances were not as greatly watched. I think soon after, the team and Brian realised that we had potential to be successful, and I think he turned his attention more towards the women. We found a belief that we could be successful. There was a definite shift in focus heading into '88."

3. PUTTING THE TEAM TOGETHER

"Of all the talking points which make international sport fascinating, selecting a team to represent the country surely takes pride of place."

British sportswriter E.W. Swanton

Those who played in Los Angeles had a long time to contemplate that game against the Netherlands and the injustice of being forced into a penalty shoot-out. The Australian team did not play another international match until 10 June 1985; a period of 304 days between matches.

By then, Loretta Dorman had been dropped. "When I came back from Los Angeles, I was dropped from the team about eight months later. I stayed a bit longer in Perth and then went back home. I think the difference for me was that I had to get back into the team. I made some big changes. I was really determined then, whereas before I was evolving as a hockey player, and I think it gave me a taste and then I just thought, 'no, I really want that'. I'd seen what you need to do to be at that level. I think it was a totally different campaign. I think the Institute had a big part to play because we were training together all the time. We had an expectation of what we needed to deliver. There were definitely a lot of people that went to Los Angeles still in the Seoul team, so they had the hunger and the fight to know what it was all about. So absolutely, one campaign definitely helped the second campaign."

As to why she was dropped, Loretta admitted that she never asked, but gave a frank assessment of her own. "I think it was just that I didn't perform. I know that I'd put on some weight. I got into the team because I was scoring goals left, right and centre, and then I just didn't cope with the travel. I just really wasn't ready for it," she said. "Looking back, it was just my level of maturity. I just didn't know how to handle it. Moving to Perth was my first time away from home, and then there was the travelling overseas. In those days, there was no English speaking in many countries like it is now. I still recall when we first got to Germany, receiving a telegram from my parents at the hotel saying, 'Hi, I hope you got there okay.' Those sorts of things are just foreign now."

That first game after Los Angeles would be played in Amsterdam's Wagener Stadium as part of a five-nation tournament, and their opening opponent was the USA. Revenge was sweet as goals from Trish Heberle and Sharon Buchanan secured a 2-1 victory.

The team then drew with Russia and lost to West Germany and the host nation, the Netherlands.

The European tour concluded with a Test match against West Germany in Bremen where the two teams played out a 0-0 draw, and then Test matches in Scotland and Great Britain. The team recorded three victories, scoring 11 goals and conceding just one against Great Britain.

The year would finish with the team playing a five-Test series against England at home but in cities around the country, followed by a similar series against West Germany. Against England they recorded four wins and a draw, while against West Germany they won four Tests and lost one.

The focus in 1986 was very much on the World Cup in August. It was being hosted by the Netherlands.

In April in Sydney, Australia hosted the Esanda International event which saw New Zealand, South Korea, Canada and the USA also compete. Australia drew and lost with the USA and defeated the other nations.

In May, the International Olympic Committee announced that it was prepared to throw away the traditional amateur eligibility criteria for Olympic competitors, making the Games open to all. The move to admit professionals came when the 11-member committee endorsed the plan to give amateurs, professionals, and State-sponsored athletes equal status. This change was voted on in October.

The Olympic authority's determination to face up to the commercial realities of modern sport would remove the remaining vestiges of the strict amateur code imposed on the modern Olympic movement 90 years ago by its founder, Baron Pierre de Coubertin. It would be the most fundamental change undertaken since the modern Games began in 1896.

Under the new regulations, the world's highest paid sports personalities would be eligible to participate in both the summer and winter Games. Athletes could finally be financially rewarded for their efforts. However, the change would not become official until the 1992 Olympic Games in Barcelona.

It was also announced that a fund of USD 4.72 million had been set aside to pay Olympic teams a minimum of USD 10,000, with individuals receiving USD 300 for competing in the Olympics. The money was to be drawn from revenue obtained from the worldwide marketing of the Olympic emblem by Swiss-based company, ISL.

ISL was established by former Adidas boss Horst Dassler and was associated with FIFA, the International Olympic Committee and the International Association of Athletics Federations. It collapsed in 2001 with debts of 153 million pounds.

The decision to allow professional athletes to compete at the Olympics had as much to do with the Olympic movement needing the revenue offered by television networks as it was about supposedly amateur athletes being paid under the table or funded by governments. To benefit from the television revenue, the television stations required the top stars to compete in the Games to ensure they received a return on their investment.

However, hockey and the athletes selected to represent Australia and many other countries would see little change in their fortunes in the next few years or decades.

In August of 1986, the Australian women played warm-up games for the World Cup against West Germany in Essen and Cologne and won both games, 2-1 and 3-1 respectively. They then defeated New Zealand and the USA in Amsterdam, 5-1 and 4-2.

This meant that their form heading into the World Cup had seen them play nine matches since the start of the year, winning seven, drawing one and losing one. Not surprisingly, the mood heading into the World Cup was extremely positive.

Elspeth Denning scored twice in the opening game against England, but the team could only draw 2-2. She scored another double a day later as Australia beat Canada 2-0.

Their third game many believed would decide who topped Pool A, with their opponent being the Netherlands who in recent times had the wood over the Australians. They did again this time. Australia went behind before Denning equalised. Then just after the halftime break, two goals in two minutes from Sophie von Weller gave the Dutch the advantage. Jackie Pereira pulled a goal back, but the Dutch prevailed 3-2.

The following day was a rest day. When the action resumed, Australia was first to play and defeated Spain 3-1 thanks to two goals from Julene Grant and one from Sharon Buchanan. England defeated Scotland 1-0, but then in the third game Canada recorded a shock victory over the Dutch 2-1. Mary Conn was the hero for the Canadians with a double.

At the start of the day, Canada had been a point ahead of Australia because of the draw against England. Now after three games, the Netherlands and Canada were top of the pool – both on six points and Australia was third with five.

Going into the final pool match, Australia needed a win and had to hope that Spain would beat the Netherlands and for England to defeat Canada to have any hope of making the medal matches.

Australia played first and scored seven unanswered goals against Scotland, with Elspeth Denning scoring a hat-trick and Debbie Bowman a brace. Then they had to sit back and watch. The Dutch beat Spain 5-0, confirming their place in the semi-final.

Heading into the last ten minutes of their game, Canada were still 0-0 with England. If the match finished in a draw, Australia would progress courtesy of a superior goal difference, even though they would be level on points with Canada.

With six minutes to go, Canada won a penalty corner, and Lisa Lyn converted to book the Canadians a semi-final berth. They would go on to claim third place and the Netherlands would win the World Cup.

Australia, again having been so close to being among the medals, had to play off for 5th and 6th after beating Russia 7-0 in a crossover match. Their opponents were England, a team they had not lost to since 1967. The match finished 2-2 and went into extra time. In the 86th minute, Karen Brown broke the deadlock and England claimed fifth spot. Australia had to settle for sixth.

The only consolation was that Elspeth Denning was equal top scorer for the tournament with Russia's Natella Krasnikova, both with nine goals.

Australian captain at the World Cup, Sandra Pisani, made headlines back home in Australia when she implied that the Dutch had deliberately lost to Canada to reduce the chances of Australia progressing to the semi-finals.

The Netherlands were accused of playing a weaker side against Canada. *"There's a lot of talk that the Dutch didn't want to win against Canada,"* Pisani was quoted in *The Advertiser* as saying. *"They didn't want to play us in the finals. We're very disappointed in that. We feel as if we have been cheated."*

"I don't want to make it sound like bad sportsmanship. I'd always thought that no one goes out to lose a game. But it does happen. Teams will get rid of a side if they think it's going to worry them in the final. We can't blame anyone but ourselves for not qualifying for the semi-finals. We should have done better in the first game than a 2-2 draw with England, especially after we killed them in Australia last year."

Did Sandy have a point? Three players that played the full game in the final were substitutes in the game against Canada and came on after the 40-minute mark.

They say that what doesn't kill you makes you stronger. Having suffered two heartbreaking tournaments, something had to change. Something needed tweaking to see this group of players fulfil their undoubted potential. They were close, but at that point in time were lacking something. They had exactly 24 months to find the answers.

Brian Glencross was given some help to prepare the players for the 1988 Seoul Olympic Games. It was clear that he had a very talented group at his disposal, but they needed something to bring out the best in them.

Two Englishmen came into the group and both in their own way would have an impact.

Peter Freitag came in as an assistant coach.

He was a former member of the England and British hockey team in 1973, '74 and '75. He had high hopes of heading to the Montreal Olympic Games in 1976. Great Britain had to face Belgium in a play-off match to determine which nation would claim the last qualification place.

"I didn't play in that match as I had injured my ribs," Peter advised, looking back on that time. "Belgium wasn't that good in those days. However, Belgium won 2-1. I was playing on the village green in Cranleigh Village when they announced the news that we had lost 2-1. I was not that injured as I was still playing. It was devastating news. We had to keep training though as we were the first reserve team should anyone withdraw. We played some practice games, I think Malaysia at Portman Road, Ipswich Town's home ground. Then the Kenyans said, 'we are not going'. So, the team of which I was a member was told to get to the airport, we are going to Montreal. This was the Saturday of the Opening Ceremony. I kissed the family goodbye and headed to Heathrow. Then at the airport we were told the Kenyans had not officially said they were not going, so we can't put you on the plane, we will have to wait and see what happens."

"So, we spent a night in a hotel at Heathrow Airport. We were all in our blazers and Bob Mason who ran GB hockey had these pennants made that he had given us. We went to bed that night thinking that we were going to the Olympic Games in the morning. Sadly, when we woke up, we were told we were not going, as Kenya still hadn't officially pulled out and it would be bad etiquette to go before that time. So, we grabbed our bags and headed home."

Freitag retired from playing in 1978 after the World Cup in Buenos Aires. "I am very glad that I did because they did not go to Moscow either," he said, "and I think that would have killed me. I can laugh about it now, but at the time, it was terrible."

So, like many of the Australian players, he knew the cruelty of sport and what disappointment felt like.

Interestingly, he was never really looking for a job with the Australian team, as he explained.

"I was teaching at Scotch College and started coaching. Hockey is one of those sports that opened doors for me. I had done a little bit of coaching in England, but had hurt my back, and so was struggling a little bit, so [I] came out to Australia. I coached a club side called Suburban Nedlands – now Suburban Lions – and we won the premiership in '82, '83 and '84. I had a good team, we did well, and I think I was doing a good job, although I know that sounds arrogant. I don't think they had won a premiership since 1930. Then I coached the State under-19 women's team, and I think we came second a couple of times, and so Shirley Davies spoke to me. She was either the President of Western Australia's Women's Hockey Association or involved with Australian women's hockey, and she said I should apply as they were looking for an assistant coach to help Brian."

"After LA where the girls had come fourth following a ridiculous play-off, they were looking for someone younger and a bit different to Brian, and someone who was based in Western Australia. It was not on a professional basis, but on a voluntary help-us-out basis. So, I decided to apply. Shirley saw my scrappy CV and told me I couldn't possibly send that in, so I redid it and applied, and they offered me the job. It was not really a job, as I was not paid and still teaching, but I would go out to the stadium two or three mornings a week, Saturday mornings and Sunday afternoons, whatever it was, to help coach."

"Brian was a hard taskmaster, and he was old school, and there was nothing wrong with that. They wanted someone a bit different, and a people person. Brian was a lovely man, and very genuine when you got to know him. Soft underneath, but on the coaching field he was hard. I think the idea was to put me in and help him to communicate better, and we would have that yin and yang thing, so that we would have a good balance. Brian was shocked. I don't think he knew me from a bar of soap, and suddenly I was foisted on him. I remember our first meeting and he was like, 'How come you are here?' It was awkward."

"Brian was focused on his hockey, very driven, his mind was one track – 'this is what we must do', and I guess I was there just to try and help get that message over to people – to help with the communication, as sometimes he could be very straightforward. I was there to help put what he wanted [to say] a different way. I think in time, we became a good team in that respect."

"The other man to come onboard was Brian Miller. As Peter Freitag explained, 'he became the psychologist of the team' and he added so much that I think he was one of the key factors. If you ever wanted to say what turned the Australian women's team around from being a good team to being a great team, Brian Miller would be one of those key factors. The reason I say that is first, he knew his psychology of sport, but also, he worked really well with Brian Glencross and myself. He was the sort of guy you could trust and bounce ideas off."

"I was working at the AIS in Canberra and I was in charge of psychology for athletics, rowing, and netball, which was fine and good, and kept me busy. But because I had done some work with hockey in the UK before coming out to Australia in 1984, somebody then said, 'Could you do something for hockey in Perth?'" was how Brian remembered the first approach for him to become involved with the hockey program.

"So, I went across to Perth a couple of times, I think it was in 1986, to work with the AIS programs. It was nice, I worked with Richard Aggiss on the men's side and Brian on the women's. They had never had much involvement with sports psychology before, and they found this quite interesting, and Richard got me involved with the men's 1986 program and getting them ready for the London World Cup."

"Brian initially was, I guess you would say he was up for it, but he had other issues that he had to deal with, and that was perfectly fine. Part of my remit was to go and talk to the various sports if they put their hand up and asked for assistance. But post the World Cup failure of 1986, Brian then came and said, 'we are in the poo here, we need to sort something out'."

"I think that he was under pressure from the board, and you have to remember the women's side was a separate entity then. I have no proof, but I have a feeling he felt that his job was on the line. The World Cup result was a major disappointment for everybody, and there were a few things going on. Back then there was a President, and she was a volunteer, and I gather she was saying one thing here and another thing there, and so understandably I think Brian ran up the white flag and said, 'we need somebody to help'. It was more or less like, 'you are someone we know, and you are as good as anybody, so you'll do'."

"I was then called over to a camp in November '86 where they had 30-odd players, after which they were going to cut it down to maybe 20 or 18. The President and other Board members were there, and there was some finger-wagging to the team, telling them 'that was a disgrace, you played badly, you also did some other stuff, so there is going to be a change'. Then I turned up," he recalled with a laugh.

The President of the Australian Women's Hockey Association (AWHA) at that time was Meg Wilson. She had played for both Tasmania and Australia, became a State umpire, and coached and managed the Australian team at the IFWHA tournament in 1975. She then moved into administration and from 1985 until 1996, she was President of the AWHA, and from 1966 to 1989 and was also President of the Tasmanian Women's Hockey Association (TWHA).

Wilson was also the first AWHA representative to be appointed to the International Hockey Federation Council (FIH) in 1986.

Her tireless efforts on behalf of the sport were not only recognised with life membership to the AWHA and TWHA, but also when she was inducted into the Sport Australia Hall of Fame as a General Member for her contribution to hockey in 1990.

Wilson passed away aged 96 on Friday, May 7, 2021. While she may well have ruffled a few feathers, she was dedicated to doing what she thought was best for the game, and in 1986 made changes that she felt were needed for this group of players and Australian hockey to fulfil its potential.

Brain Miller had no idea what he was walking into. "I didn't know any of the background, I just rocked up to that camp," he remembered, before revealing that one of the first issues he was to be involved with was the appointment of a new captain.

"Sandy Pisani was the captain at that stage, and they were already saying [that] she can't be the captain anymore," Miller explained. "That came right from the top, from the Board. She can stay on as a player, but not as captain."

Prior to his arrival, discussions had already been taking place, as Debbie Bowman remembered. "I had no aspirations to be captain. Brian came up to me one day and said we have a few people, I think it was five, that we are thinking we would like to offer the position of captain to. Are you interested? That was it basically."

"I said I need to think about it. I went back to my partner and asked him, and he said, 'Well how do you feel?' I said, 'I don't know, I suppose I am happy to put my hat in the ring, but I am not sure.'"

"I had been captain for my club and State teams, so I had had a captaincy role since I was a child. So, I thought, well you've captained everything else so why not put your hand in, so I put my hand up."

As Miller explained, he hit the ground running. "It was, 'you have got to find a new captain, and you have to get rid of one or two other players'. I think some of the older ones may have been involved in some of the controversial stuff. I never knew what that was, but there was talk that alcohol was involved, and there was apparently some incident, but who knows? Frankly I didn't really care, this was a new broom. There were some new kids coming through like Sally Carbon and Rechelle Hawkes who came into the squad, and part of that was to say, 'we are having a reset here'."

By the time that Miller arrived at the camp, the captaincy had already been narrowed down to two candidates – Sharon Buchanan and Debbie Bowman. As the new team psychologist, Miller was asked to meet with both and share his thoughts with Glencross.

"I didn't know any of these people. To me, they were a lovely bunch of athletes all running around. Basically, they had said, 'It was either going to be Sharon or Debbie, can you interview them and give me your opinion?' So, I did, and they both seemed really good, they gave all the right answers to all the questions, so I told Brian, and he told the President that they both seemed good candidates. I certainly did not say that one was better than the other, as I really didn't know them, and I only had about 30 minutes with each of them. They could clearly both play hockey. I suspect that in the end, Brian made the final choice, but he could almost have been given instructions from on high. To my mind it wouldn't have mattered, it was a toss-up between the two as both seemed pretty good."

"It was a good platform for me to come into from a purely selfish point of view, as they had gone to the World Cup ranked around number two and had had a bit of a disaster, but were clearly still pretty bloody good at playing hockey, so the only way was up."

Debbie Bowman was announced as the captain in November of 1986.

It was not going to be easy, but looking back, Bowman believes that she was aware of the task she was taking on.

"I think my personality came into play and I think back to when I was at school and even then, I was never in a situation where I needed to get along with a certain group. So, when it came to the girls, I never became involved with any individual as such. I never befriended anyone for any reason, nor did I dislike someone for whatever reason. My personality, and maybe it was my hairdressing, I don't know, but I tended to go with the flow. I never got into the politics, I allowed them to have their views, and I was there to train. That was basically it."

"I never took the captaincy on thinking I was the leader of this team, as there were so many leaders. They didn't need another leader. They were individual personalities, some very strong individual personalities, to very quiet ones. So, I just went along saying, 'I am here to focus on my training', I would listen to what Brian Miller had to say and listen to what the coaches said and then try and lead by example. My leadership was focused on 'do the right thing, give 100% and come off the field', and there were times I didn't even know what the score was. People would come off at halftime upset and say, 'look at the score' and I would say, 'what is the score?' I just had this thing of focusing on your job and doing it the best you can, and everyone doing that and playing as a team. If we did that, it would all fall into place. If we all play as a team, we are all going to be successful."

Despite feeling that Bowman or Buchanan were ideal candidates for the captaincy, Brian Miller conceded that it was no easy task. "I think it did end up where Debbie was a bit separate because she was the captain, and I think that did make life tough, and there was definitely friction. There was the 'WA gang' as they were known and she was a Queenslander, so there was all that stuff."

Miller paused before admitting, "from a selfish high-performance point of view, I wasn't unhappy, because what I didn't want was sixteen best mates, which I know is what some people have gone on to describe it as. I can tell you that it definitely wasn't that. There has to be a little bit of needle, but it must be controlled. You would often find a situation where Debbie and Maree would have a different opinion to the other 14 players, and that is OK as long as you manage it. Saying that, you do not want 15 against one, that is never good!"

Many have debated what it is that sets world-class teams apart. Is it key players coming together at the same time? Is it the coach? There is no definitive answer. However, those who have been part of such teams will tell you there are a number of factors that contribute to that success. Interestingly "luck" is a word that frequently comes up. That in major tournaments or games, you need to have an element of luck go your way, be it key players not being injured, a shot hitting the post rather than going in, or a key decision at a key moment going your team's way.

Other words used include "coherence" in terms of purpose and belief. Coaches will tell their players that they must believe in order to achieve. Today that is often called "vision". Vision is not to be confused with an objective, as every team has an objective. Vision is linked to something far greater. It is a big picture, something that all involved see and share. Not only that, but it must also bring an emotional attachment which excites.

However, despite having a shared vision, goal or purpose, few great teams live in perfect harmony.

Brian Miller has stated that despite the way it has been portrayed, this was a squad with differences, which was a good thing as a harmonious squad can be a recipe for disaster. "As ever in any team, there is task cohesion and social cohesion, and lots of work has been done over the years in high-performance sport that you want a team in sport to be 100% task cohesive, but if they are 100% socially cohesive where everybody loves everybody, that is a disaster."

Top players and top teams are often extremely self-critical, and in the modern day far more analytical than they were back in the 1980s. However, this was a change that Miller brought to the team.

One crucial component of great teams is effectively managing those different personalities and talents both on and off the field of play. There needs to be a balance between managing these issues that is shared between the coach and the captain.

Many successful teams will reflect and come to the conclusion that a key component was that the captain was an extension of the coach on the field of play. That the two must have a shared vision as well as shared beliefs about how the team must function.

According to Brian Miller, this may well have been the reason that Debbie Bowman was chosen by Brian Glencross. "She was very much the conduit to that professionalism on the pitch when the game was underway. That probably didn't help in terms of her popularity, but it was vital in terms of what was best for the team."

He then gave an example of that leadership. "Some of the first few matches when I watched the team play, I noticed that if there was an injury, and the doctor was on the pitch or there was some lull for two or three minutes, there would be two or three girls over there and two or three in another area, which to me was unprofessional. So, we changed the system so that if that happened, they all got together in a central place to have a chat or a drink and get their heads together. It was hardly rocket science. Brian would send a signal to Debbie where he would point one way to talk about attack, or the other way to talk about defence, or tap his head to have her talk about attitude. Debbie had to interpret Brian's signals, and then speak to the team for as long as it took, always keeping an eye on the umpires and physios to pace and time her talk. So, it was quite a difficult task."

Bowman herself admitted that she loved the tactical side of a game and, like many of her male counterparts, would enjoy studying games. "I was very tactical. My whole upbringing in hockey was [that] I saw it very much as a chess game, and Brian and I were very similar in the way that we thought. It was like if that person moved there, what was going to happen on the other side of the field, and if someone did something else here, what will the reaction be? There must be a chain reaction as a result of that happening, and I loved that. I think Brian also instilled a lot of my thought processes when it came to that."

"Plus, the boys, the Australian men, Peter Haselhurst, who played my position, he was like that. He was an analytical player. Ric Charlesworth was the same. They would spend hours going over and over an incident. This will sound silly, but I would draw in the steam on the glass of my shower a hockey field and go if that is going to happen there, what will happen with Smally out on the right wing, or Lee on the left wing? I would be playing these scenarios all the time and had done for a very long time. So that is where I think Brian and I connected very, very, well."

Brian Glencross's assistant coach Peter Freitag also backed up that from the coach's perspective, Bowman was the ideal person for the job, but that it was far from easy.

"Debbie was not a popular captain in some respects," he said, before adding, "we liked her as coaches because she was a workhorse who simply worked and worked. She may have lacked the flair skills of Rechelle Hawkes, but she would run, and she was gutsy."

He then related a story which showed how hard it was initially. "She spoke at a press conference and said, 'my team', and the girls all took umbrage at that, which baffled me. As it was her team, she was the captain. It's a phrase that you use when you are captain."

"Sometimes she could be blunt and that would sometimes not go down too well with some of the girls," he added. "She also wasn't a WA girl, and there were a lot of them in the team. We liked her, she was a mature person, she led by example, and she worked her butt off for the team."

Freitag also remembered another aspect that Brian Miller brought to the team which he could relate to from his time as an England international.

"When Brian came in, I remember him telling the players to practise how you carry yourself. We want to be confident and assertive. The girl's response was, 'oh, but we don't want to be arrogant'. He explained that it was not about being arrogant, but about being assertive, so that when you walk into the room, it's 'I am an Australian international hockey player, I am somebody'."

"They found that quite hard. I was able to relate to this because when I was playing for England, we went to the World Cup in '75 in Kuala Lumpur. At a reception, I remember the Indian team came in wearing their turbans and their blazers, and we were intimidated. I remember it clearly. We were like, 'ahh that's Ajit Pal Singh...' and it was game over. Who did we play in the first game? India, we lost comfortably 2-1, and it could have been 10-0," Freitag recalled.

"We practised it, like a roleplay, and the girls loved it, and more importantly, they loved him. Brian Miller gave the girls that confidence. He was a very good foil for Brian Glencross and for me too. He knew his sport and the complexities of winning, and we talked about goals and who we were, and why we were here. I think he was a key factor in getting us to have the right winning mindset. I don't think anyone would underestimate the role he played."

There was another shift that was implemented as soon as Brian Miller came on board. "One of the worst things that I came into at that November camp was there would be hundreds of hockey balls on the practice field, and there would be Peter Freitag and Brian [Glencross] going around picking up the last half dozen balls or so," Miller recalled. "The coaches were doing everything even as far as picking up and bringing in the balls. I said, 'no, that is not what happens'. It was important to go, 'you, you, and you today, you are in charge of that'. The players had a sense that everything would be done and organised for them, and I came back to this point: 'you have never won anything, you can expect that when you are successful', but they were incredibly confident."

Although he explained that this system did not always work. "In 1992 when I was working with team GB, we turned up at a match and no one brought the balls from the hotel, so it didn't always work out for the best!"

There can be no doubt that Miller was accepted from that very first camp and was soon accepted as part of the team by all.

"What I did during that first training camp that I came into, which lasted for about 10 days, was I had one-to-one sessions with most of the players; I am not sure I spoke to all of them, but certainly most of them. In those sessions, I just asked a few questions and then they came up with their stories, and their versions of the truth, and they were all kind of saying, 'this is not good enough'. I also think in part because the men had just won their World Cup, and my contribution to that was modest, it was almost as if there was a view that OK, that must work," he modestly explained, before adding, "the thing was with the girls, most teams you work with or even individual athletes coming in, most psychologists will tell you the number one thing to work on is their confidence. I rocked up, and bearing in mind they had come 5th or 6th at the World Cup, their confidence was sky high. I couldn't get my brain around it initially, as I was thinking, 'You have never won anything, how can you be so confident?' But they were, which was good for me."

Over the next year, a great deal of work was done by all to turn that confidence into success.

"We added a little one per cent here and another one per cent there," Miller explained. "So, they were becoming more professional. Some of them really bought into it and really loved everything we were doing, and that was really good. Some of them didn't as much, but that is the same with any team you work with, so that is OK. But they definitely, and not just because of me but because there was someone there carrying out that role, they were better prepared than they had ever been before because they were dealing with professionalism issues which they had paid lip service to before."

The team played their last game at the World Cup on 23 August 1986; however, a great amount of work was being done behind the scenes to ensure that come the '88 Olympic Games, this group of players finally fulfilled their potential.

Unlike the modern day, after the World Cup the year before they would not take the field again until 15 June 1987 when they were back in Amsterdam and the Wagener Stadium for two Test matches against the USA. This was 296 days between international games.

The first Test was won 2-1, the second a day later was lost by the same scoreline.

The team was in the Netherlands for the subsequent BMW Champions Trophy. The six teams competing were the Netherlands, Australia, South Korea, Canada, Great Britain and New Zealand.

On day one, Australia thumped New Zealand 8-0 with hat-tricks to Jackie Pereira and Kim Small. Korea defeated Canada 4-0 and the Netherlands beat Great Britain by the same score.

On days two and three, Great Britain bounced back to beat New Zealand 5-0 while the Netherlands beat Canada 4-1 and Australia beat South Korea 3-1, Pereira with a double and Small with the other goal.

Australia and the hosts the Netherlands were the only two unbeaten teams and they continued their winning ways with Australia beating Great Britain 1-0 and the Netherlands taking care of South Korea 5-0, and the next day New Zealand 4-0.

Australia drew their penultimate game against Canada 1-1. This meant that the final game between the Netherlands and Australia would determine who finished top of the ladder and claimed the Champions Trophy.

It would be no easy game for Australia. The Dutch had scored 17 goals in their four games and conceded just one against Canada.

The Dutch took a 2-0 lead in the first half with Sophie von Weller and Lisanne Lejeune scoring. In the second half, two goals in a minute from Elspeth Denning and Jackie Pereira pulled Australia level. However, it wasn't to be as Lejeune scored her second goal before Helena van der Ben wrapped the game up with a fourth. Australia had to settle for the silver medal.

Jackie Pereira was also pipped for the top goal scorer award, as South Korea's Lim Kye-Sook scored four in their final game against New Zealand to finish with eight goals to Pereira's seven.

Following the Champions Trophy, Brian Glencross urged Sandy Pisani to leave her home city of Adelaide to be exposed to stiffer competition, although the playing surface may well have been another reason for the coach's comments. *"She's not getting that in Adelaide where she can't play on wet, artificial pitches. She needs to get tough competition all the time to keep improving,"* Brian was quoted in the press as saying.

The team would have one more outing before the end of 1987 and that was in a four-nation tournament at the Olympic venue. It was a test event to ensure that all was in place for the Olympic Games the following year.

Australia played the USA once and South Korea twice. Despite it being a four-nation tournament, only three participated. No one seemed to remember the reason why.

In the first game against South Korea, Australia won 4-3 with Angie Lambert scoring two, and Pereira and Sally Carbon the others.

This was Carbon's debut tournament, as she explained. "There's no doubt that I came in at the absolute perfect time. The reason why I got in was because Sharon Buchanan retired in '87. So, I slotted into Sharon's spot, and then, of course, she came back. She reversed her retirement about six months later and came back, so someone else had to drop out at that point in time. So, that was quite an interesting way to get in. The other thing that was interesting in our early days in the side was that both Rechelle Hawkes and I, Western Australians, we got into the Australian squad before we broke into the Western Australian team. This was because we had so many Western Australians who were either still playing for Australia or had just finished their Australian career but were still very good and in the State team, and you can't drop an '84 Olympian to pull in this 'maybe' youngster. So, we did it arse about face didn't we? We did it the wrong way around, but it obviously worked. My first game was exactly one year before the Olympics in Seoul. It was at the Seoul preparation tournament."

Carbon remembered scoring not only on debut, but also with her first touch. "I ran onto the field. My first touch of the ball ever in my Australian career, I got a goal! I just played excited. I was just like, 'woohoo, this is seriously fun', and obviously the rest of the year was just as much fun." A smile spread across her face as she said this, and a laugh followed.

Their second game was a 2-1 win over the USA before they played a 4-4 draw with South Korea in their second meeting. This time Liane Tooth grabbed a brace and Lee Capes and Kim Small grabbed the other two goals.

There was then a long break between matches with the team seeing no action for four months until just before the Bicentennial Tournament in Perth. This event coincided with celebrations across the country as Australia celebrated its 200th anniversary. There they would face many of the same teams they had faced in the Champions Trophy

Just prior to this tournament, there were two Test matches against the USA played at Christchurch Grammar School. Australia went down 2-1 in the opening game but won the second 2-0.

Their opening game at the Bicentennial Tournament was a 5-1 victory over trans-Tasman rivals New Zealand where Lee Capes and Deborah Bowman grabbed two goals each and Jackie Pereira one.

A 3-1 victory followed over South Korea, then a 1-0 win over Great Britain. Next up were Canada who had in recent times proved a tough nut to crack, but Australia threw the form book out of the window with an emphatic 5-2 victory. Debbie Bowman bagged a hat-trick, and Elspeth Denning and Kim Small scored the other goals.

The final game, just as it had been in Amsterdam almost eight months to the day at the Champions Trophy earlier in the year, was against the Netherlands. A team Australia had not beaten since 15 October 1983 in the last Test match of a five-Test series. That had been their only win in the previous ten meetings.

On this occasion, goals from Tracey Belbin and Elspeth Denning were enough for Australia to record a 2-1 victory. It was a victory that possibly few at the time realised would be so important.

Going through this tournament undefeated put the team in a good position with the Olympic Games just six months away.

One of the key things prior to the Games was picking a squad. "That has been one of the hardest things throughout my career as a coach and a selector," Brian Glencross admitted, "how to announce a national team. People say pin names on the board and be ready at two o'clock in the afternoon, or it goes through the radio, or in my day you had to call up the CEO of hockey and they would tell you if you were in the team or not. If they told you that you weren't in the team, you weren't allowed to ask any questions, and the CEO may not have known much about hockey anyway. It's a tough call as the sport [has] progressed. It's got harder to do, because the kudos has grown so strong, professionalism, even though it is minor to some other sports, it's still pretty devastating for people not selected. Also, what happens is because you become a squad you become close-knit; the people who were selected became quite sad because their mates didn't get selected, so there was a pressure situation that occurred again."

In May, the National Championships were held in Canberra. All of the squad knew that this was where the team for the Olympic Games would be selected.

The cream of Australia's women hockey players gathered in Canberra for the 1988 Esanda Australian Women's Hockey Championships at the Australian Institute of Sport. Joint favourites were Western Australia and New South Wales who had met in the grand final the year before, with Western Australia winning 2-1. That victory was even more remarkable as Western Australia's first gathering of their complete team was on the plane on the way to the event! In the previous three National Championships, there had never been more than a one goal difference between the two States.

In 1988, the admission charge was $2 per day for adults and children were free. Season tickets were available for $10.

Coach Colin Brandis had a wealth of talent at his disposal for Western Australia and stated prior to the tournament that one of his biggest problems as a coach was having "sixteen outstanding players and only eleven positions". He also revealed that he would be using a penalty-corner combination of Sharon Patmore (Buchanan), Michelle Capes and Elspeth Denning as he "can see no reason to change the successful Australian combination".

One player who was involved with the national team but missing from South Australia's squad at the Championships was Sandy Pisani. She was in Canberra acting as assistant coach to the team despite her State being in desperate need of her services to help them progress to the semi-finals. Pisani, regarded as one of the most dynamic midfielders in Australian hockey, had been sidelined since March with a posterior cruciate ligament tear.

Coach Jane Lamprey told *The Canberra Times*: "*Sandy's got to the point where she can do work on her knee, but it's only safe for her to do straight line work, no twisting or rapid acceleration. She's got Olympic commitments to consider at this stage, and although we would otherwise be tempted to throw her in against Victoria, Australia needs her in Seoul more desperately than we need her here.*"

Victoria would claim the Esanda National Championship title in 1988 ending a dominant period for Western Australia who had won 11 titles since 1974 losing in 1978 and 1980 to South Australia and 1985 and 1988 to Victoria.

The Australian team named at the conclusion of the women's hockey championships was to all intents and purposes the team that would represent Australia at the Seoul Olympics. However, protocol prevented the Australian Women's Hockey Association from calling the team "the Olympic team" at that point in time, as the selections had to be ratified by the Australian Olympic Federation.

Despite announcing the team in May there were not expected to be any changes made to the side before the Games began in September.

"At the end of the National Championships, they had all the State teams lined up out on the field and then they called out those who had been selected for the Olympics," Lee Capes recalled. "I remember because it was Capes, and I am Lee, and my sister Michelle was after me alphabetically. So, when I heard my name, I walked forward but there wasn't elation because I was still waiting to hear her name read out. Once I heard her name and knew that she was picked as well, that was when I could celebrate."

Sister Michelle was picked and admitted that she was unaware of her sister's concerns. She just assumed that they would play together. "We were born on the same day but five years apart and I think because we've played hockey together for so long, it was just always a natural thing for us to be on trips together and, yeah, travel together and it was always great having your sister on the same team. I just went with whatever was going on and loved playing and loved travelling. Then the Olympics came. It was one thing came after the next type of thing. I wanted to get selected for the Olympics, but I just wanted to play. I loved travelling with those girls, and loved playing with all those girls, loved training with all those girls, and whatever benefits came with it was an added plus I guess."

Jackie Pereira was another who remembered how the selection was announced. "It was in alphabetical order, so if you didn't hear your name where it should be, that meant that you hadn't been selected. So, if we were successful, or if you failed to be selected, you failed in front of the whole hockey community. It wasn't the best way to do it, but I guess whatever way you do it is never going to be easy to let people know. I know another time you had to call the Hockey Association to find out, and another time they rang you. They have tried all different ways but if you are not picked, no way is a good way, is it?"

While some players were left standing nervously in the middle of Bruce Field waiting to hear their name read out, Liane Tooth admitted that she was quietly confident that she would hear hers.

"I think by the time they picked the team for '88, I was reasonably confident. Obviously, you can never be 100 per cent sure, but I was probably happy with the way I'd been playing and the like. So, I felt fairly well-established, and felt fairly confident that I was going to be selected. But I'm sure there've been many people that have been fairly confident they were going to be selected in teams and then receive a rude shock." Liane did not receive a shock. Her name was read out.

Lorraine Hillas had been a part of the team in 1984 and had watched the squad evolve over the next four years. Once she heard her name called out, she admitted that she felt confident the side would do well. "I think that the '88 team was essentially very different from that '84 team. The next four years saw a lot of retirements, so there were some new faces in '88. I can remember saying to Michelle Capes once when she asked, 'How do you think we'll go?' I said, 'I actually think we could get a medal, and we could get gold.' She was like, 'Oh really?'"

Elspeth Denning also felt that there were no surprises when the team was announced. "I think the team had been together for a while and it pretty much picked itself. There were a couple of players who may have surprised a few people, but I don't think they surprised us. Leading into the Olympics, the closer the Games got, and once the team was named, we became even closer. That is always the hardest time when the team is picked, as you feel for teammates that have been left out, but I think in '88 it pulled us all closer together."

"I can't even remember the announcement," Sally Carbon stated with a laugh. "The only thing I can remember is that my Mum and Dad were there, and Dad bought me and the team a really big champagne bottle. He bought a magnum, and it was probably the first time that my Dad had ever given me a drink of alcohol, or anything that even represents something slightly naughty, and that's what I can remember more than the fact that I got in the Olympic team. You know that Mum and Dad were obviously very excited, whereas I was still on this ride of absolute joy."

This is the team that was announced (in alphabetical order):

Tracey Belbin (QLD)
Debbie Bowman (QLD)
Sharon Buchanan (WA)
Lee Capes (WA)
Michelle Capes (WA)
Sally Carbon (WA)
Elspeth Denning (WA)
Loretta Dorman (ACT)
Maree Fish (TAS)
Rechelle Hawkes (WA)
Lorraine Hillas (QLD)
Kathleen Partridge (NSW)
Jackie Pereira (WA)
Sandy Pisani (SA)
Kim Small (NSW)
Liane Tooth (NSW)

Budding Australian selectors had also had the chance to pick their side for the Olympic Games in a competition organised by the Australian Women's Hockey Association. The first correct entry drawn from a barrel was declared the winner, and the competition was supervised by the Director of Management of the Australian Women's Hockey Association, Rosemary Nicholson. (Unfortunately, we could not find the name of the winner).

At the end of the tournament, it was also announced that the Australian women's hockey team had received second seeding for the Olympics, and the Australian men's team was seeded number one. Needless to say, the media of the day started talking up Australia becoming a dual-medal winning country in hockey. Not only that, but the possibility of dual gold medals.

Prior to the Olympic Games, the team headed to Europe for two Test matches in England followed by a four-nation tournament in Germany as their final preparation for the Games in September.

Prior to leaving Australia, there were a few injury concerns in the defensive line. Sandy Pisani and Liane Tooth were recovering from injuries, and having missed the National Championships, Pisani played her first game for two months at the start of June, as did Liane Tooth who had severely sprained her ankle ligaments playing at the National Championships.

Chris Dobson flew across to Perth as a back-up following impressive performances at full back for Victoria in the National Championships. Dobson was 21 and had been a scholarship holder at the AIS in 1987 but was not invited to return in 1988. She returned to Melbourne, found a job, and got on with playing as well as she could. She played well enough to be named player of the tournament in Canberra.

Australia could not do without the experience of Tooth and Pisani in defence as it was a key component of the team. By moving to Perth, Dobson put herself in the reckoning if either did not recover, although as one newspaper reported: *"She has never played a full international, and the Olympics would be the last tournament where a sane coach would blood new recruits. She will have to capture exceptional form to oust a member of the current trio on merit."*

Coach Brian Glencross was no doubt grateful for the cover and made that clear when he was quoted as saying, *"Chris' decision reflects her professional attitude and the importance of training with the national team: if anything unfortunate happens, we're covered. The more players we get here, the better."*

Dobson quit her job to head back to Perth. This was nothing new to those who wished to play for Australia.

At the time, eight members of the Australian team were either unemployed or underemployed. The requirement to train in the morning until 9am and then again from 4.30pm made it hard to find a full-time job and an understanding employer.

Unemployment benefits were not available to the players. The "work test" as it was called then required applicants to be actively looking and ready for work. With the lifestyle that the players had, this was not feasible.

Incredibly, the players' predicament was described as simply a "by-product of the dedication now required at the national level".

Unlike some other nations, Australia didn't have a government or other institutions ready to employ their athletes. So, to compete on the world stage and have any chance of being among the medallists, not only did Australian athletes have to be good, but they had to be committed to financial sacrifice.

"We got nothing, and also what was quite troubling was we had no sponsors either," Jackie Pereira remembered. "So, we were borrowing or using uniforms that had been used in another tournament because they could not afford new uniforms every time we played. This was because we didn't have the sponsorship. Even after we won in Seoul, we were still struggling to get sponsorship. It was all a bit sad in those times, but you can kind of understand in 1988 in women's sport, you were not really going to get the funding that you required for a team that over the years did so well."

"Hockey was recognised a little bit in the paper and a little on the news if we went away for a tournament, but there wasn't a lot, and then it dropped off and you saw nothing for a long time. It's coming back a little bit now. It seems if no other sport is doing particularly well, we will get a run, but if all the other teams and sports are doing well, we get forgotten."

"With Seoul and being the Olympics, we were given uniforms that came from Adidas who sponsored the Australian Olympic team. So, we had our playing gear then. But after we won the gold medal, we had to use the same uniforms again as we weren't given any new uniforms or any other playing gear or windcheaters or anything like that! We weren't well looked after when we played. We did not have to pay for any of our travel, but while we weren't losing money, we certainly weren't making any!"

Prior to heading to Europe, Australia found itself in the spotlight. The defeat of the Dutch at the Bicentennial Tournament in Perth had made other nations sit up and take notice, wondering whether the dominant Dutch could be toppled again in Seoul. So, it was not just the Australian public who were interested in the performances of the team as they set off on their six-match tour of England and Germany.

Not best pleased with all the attention, Brian Glencross played a straight bat to the media when he said before the team left: "All the teams we will meet will be strong, that's a bonus, and it will be important to gauge the West Germans, who we haven't seen for some time. At the World Cup in 1986, we finished sixth behind a second-placed German team, and it's important to remember that they remain a formidable side. We defeated Great Britain 1-0 and Canada 5-2 in the Esanda tournament in Perth, so there's a need to practise our game against those sides and maintain our edge."

On 9 June, the team headed to Europe. On the eve of their opening game against England in Marlow, *The Canberra Times* carried an article on the Capes sisters. It advised that *"they were sharing things as they have done for most of their lives. Lee, 26, and Michelle, 21, were each selected for their first Olympics last month and have followed their mother and her sister into the Australian team."*

"It started in childhood when the girls began playing the game, under the watchful eye of their mother June, who played for Australia in 1957, six years before their Aunt Shirley played in the national team."

"The sisters live together, and they each have a relationship with an Australian men's hockey player. Michelle is engaged to Australian men's forward Mark Hager, and Lee's boyfriend is former Australian midfielder Michael Nobbs."

"Michelle and Lee played their first games for Australia on the same day, shortly after the Los Angeles Olympics. They both play on the left side of the field: Lee at wing, and Michelle at half. In 1987, they both had part-time scholarships at the AIS."

"The sisters agree they are a good combination. There is a natural understanding, and frankness."

"Their mother first saw the duo play for Australia in March at the Esanda Bicentennial Tournament in Perth, when Australia rattled off its best international performance, taking the gold medal from Holland and earning Olympic favouritism. Cautious not to break the family sequence, she will go to Seoul too."

In the opening game of the European tour, Australia put six past England, with Lee Capes claiming one. The other goals were scored by Jackie Pereira, Rechelle Hawkes, Sharon Buchanan and two to Kim Small.

The next day, they met Great Britain and played out a 1-1 draw.

From there, it was onto Essen in Germany. After a day's travel, they were back on the pitch facing Great Britain again in the four-nations tournament. This time, goals from Sharon Buchanan and Jackie Pereira ensured a 2-0 victory.

The following day the team met Canada and recorded a 2-1 victory with Pereira scoring again along with Tracey Belbin.

The final game was the next day. So, they played three games in three days, and had played five games in six days.

The team's unbeaten run, which stretched back to March when they lost to the USA in Perth, came to an end in their last game before they headed to Seoul. West Germany won a hard-fought encounter, 1-0.

Once back in Australia, preparations continued. Brian Glencross and his team were going to leave nothing to chance. They prepared for every eventuality, as Sally Carbon explained.

"One of the biggest things I can remember in preparation, this is probably when it became real, we all lived around the Hockey Stadium because we had to get there very early in the morning for training. We had to get to the stadium at 5.30am as you do for training, and then they piled us into two buses. They were 10-person buses and they drove the two buses in convoy to Floreat to the beach, and then turned around and drove us back to the stadium because that represented the time it took to get to your games every day in Seoul. They were preparing us, and as we were driving down Empire Avenue, which was so close to our home, I was thinking to myself, 'God, this is just where I've come from', we got pulled over by the Federal Police. They pulled us over, they man-handled us, they made us take all our gear off the bus, they made us empty our gear, and we have a lot of gear."

"Every piece was thrown all over the grass on the side of a busy road, and they were not being very pleasant to us at all. Then we all had to pack our stuff up, and that's probably a half-an- hour problem. Then they had us get back on the bus and they said, 'right, you're right to go'. They also had those mirror trolleys, so they'd look for bombs under our bus. They did everything and we had no idea what this was, but in hindsight it was all training, preparation for what was going to happen in Seoul, and that intensity and pressure."

"So, we headed back to training and because we were so late to training, they told us on the buses that we needed to warm up and stretch on the bus and be prepared. So, we all got our shin pads on and everything, ready to go straight into training because we were going to miss the first half hour of training."

They knew that once in Seoul, anything could happen. If Australia's game against the host nation became crucial to the hosts, then who knew what may occur if the locals tried to give their team the upper hand. Preparation such as this could have proven crucial.

On 19 August, the team flew to Canberra and the Australian Institute of Sport because the surface at Bruce Field was Poligras, the same one that would be used in Seoul. The men's team flew in a day later for similar reasons.

This final camp would also simulate the Seoul Olympic Village conditions. When the teams took to the field, recorded Korean crowd noise and music would be played at high volume through speakers around the pitch. This was done in all the trial matches to try and replicate conditions in the Olympic Stadium.

The women's team played matches against a mixed team put together by ACT men's coach Ray Dorsett, while the men's team played against an Esanda XI of past and future Australian players who were flown in for the occasion.

This camp was far from a holiday, it was serious business. According to *The Canberra Times, "a full program of seminars, videos and team talks will be held during the week, followed by the official pre-Olympic camp for the entire Australian Olympic team at the weekend."*

One distraction had the team read the Australian papers was the media's apparent obsession with the food in Korea. *"Dog soup off the menu for Olympics"* was the headline from one Reuters report.

The same report stated: *"Authorities in South Korea, sensitive to the country's image in the world spotlight during the Olympics, are forcing hundreds of dogmeat restaurants and traders in and around Seoul to close as foreigners pour in for the Games."*

Bosintang, a health soup, has boiled, shredded dog as its main ingredient.

The meat is boiled with vegetables such as green onions, perilla leaves and dandelions, as well as spices. The dish has a long history in Korean culture and is savoured by many South Koreans as an energy-enhancer, a boost for pregnant women and a cure for ills. The fact that the Koreans ate an animal that is seen as a domestic pet seemed to take up a great deal of the Australian media's attention.

In the minds of the coaches, all that could be done in preparation had been done. Now they would find out if all their efforts had been worthwhile.

The team headed to Seoul where they would play two warm-up games. The first against the USA on 15 September and the second on the 19th against Argentina. Then they would play their opening game of the tournament on the 21st.

The team that boarded the plane was the same as the one that had been announced following the National Championships in Canberra. The two reserves who would be left at home and called if required were Cheryl Moss, a half back from Queensland, and Victorian full back Chris Dobson, who had both trained with the squad in that final camp in Canberra.

Chris Dobson would play at an Olympic Games four years later in Barcelona. That appearance by the Windangs Hockey Club player made her the first female Olympian from Shepparton in Victoria.

Dobson would play 55 times for Australia while Moss would make 19 appearances.

The 16 players selected came from all around Australia and of the eight States and Territories, 6 were represented by a player in the squad. The exceptions were Victoria and the Northern Territory.

Tracey Belbin

Tracey was born on 24 June 1967 in Cairns in Far North Queensland. Before she started school, the family moved to Townsville, just under 350 km south of Cairns. It was here that she started playing hockey.

"I've got three sisters. My two older sisters started playing, and I had to go and watch them train. So, I thought, 'oh well I may as well join in', and I started playing hockey before I went to school. I was only four years old," Tracey explained. She started playing at the West Hockey club, but her time there would be short-lived.

"We moved to Mackay when I was nine, and then from Mackay I went to the AIS in Perth."

Tracey's progress was fast, as she revealed. "I played under-12 State titles, and I got selected quite young. So, I was in our senior squad I think in 1982/'83 roughly. I was only 14 or 15 years old. It was from that tournament that I went on to make the Australian squad. So, just before Los Angeles ('84 Olympics) I made the Australian squad, so I was very young. I was kind of on the radar from playing Queensland under-21s at Nationals and Queensland school sports under-16s, and then in the senior team as well. I guess Brian did his scouting probably at the Nationals and I think that was how I was on his radar."

While some of her teammates did not consider representing Australia, Tracey admitted that from a young age, she thought that one day she would.

"Part of being identified in like a talent squad or something, I don't know whether it was through schools or through Queensland Hockey, but Pam Glossop and Lorraine Hillas actually came along, and they did a coaching session with us, and Gloss had this rain jacket on with the Australian logo, and I remember thinking, 'oh that's really cool, I really want one of those'. So, I thought, 'wow, I think I should really train hard and play for Australia and get one of those jackets, because that's a really cool jacket'. My motivation was a jacket! When I got the jacket, they were these thin piss-weak little coats that wouldn't keep the rain off or anything, but I was just so proud to finally get that jacket," she admitted with a laugh.

"I was clearly young at that camp, and apart from the coat, I always aspired to play for Australia, and once you get a sniff of it, I guess, then you can say to yourself, 'well, that might be possible, I can actually play for Australia and go to an Olympics. If I go to an Olympics well, of course, you don't go for anything less than a gold medal.'"

Having made her debut leading up to the 1984 Los Angeles Olympic

Games, Tracey was given a hint that she was in the mix for selection, even though she missed out.

"It was quite weird actually because I got a call telling me I had to go and get fitted out for an Olympic uniform. I think it was in Brisbane, and I had to get fitted out in the walking-out uniform. I was only really young, but I thought, 'oh well, I've been a little bit in the mix, just imagine...' but really, I never thought I could really go. It was like, 'wow, imagine if I could go, , or something happened, and I did go'. At that time, it was more that kind of mindset."

Tracey moved to Perth and the AIS in 1985 and from that moment on, she established herself in the team.

However, it wasn't at all easy, as she explained. "It was a big adjustment. I had to reflect after talking to some of the current players and I said, 'wow, they've had 20 years of this not very nice experience', and then when I thought about it, well, mine wasn't really a bed of roses either. I just kind of got on with it because I really wanted to play. We're a pretty close family, and I left them behind and I went from a small town to Perth. I wanted to study, I aspired to study, and started at Curtin University over there as a medical laboratory technician. Then I found out that I just didn't have time. I think I was in the under-19 and under-21 Queensland teams, and the national teams. So, I just didn't have time to commit to study. So that was difficult. It was a whole new environment. We lived in dorms at Noalimba."

"I left in '87. I just went in and told Brian that 'I'm leaving and you're paying for my car to get back home'. They put it on the train and I left. That was obviously a really crucial point in time, and I came back to Brisbane and played with St Andrews. This was right before the Olympics, so obviously he had concerns about what I'd do or what work I'd do. Jan Hadfield, she was the coach of Saints at the time, and she was fantastic. I was able to live with her and to train with St Andrews, and we had a great team with great people. I think I went out of an environment where I felt stifled a little bit, to one where I was able to still train at a high level but do other things like study and work."

To some, this move may well have been the end of their Olympic dream, but Tracey never felt that way.

"I didn't think of it like I was sacrificing anything. You don't think that when you're in a situation that you feel is not conducive to your wellbeing. I wouldn't say that I had mental health issues or anything. I was away from my boyfriend at the time. I was away from my friends. Of course, I had good friends in Perth, but there wasn't work, I wasn't really working. We could pick up things, like I did some waitressing or work in a clothes store, but for me it wasn't fulfilling enough, and that's the thing you have to weigh up. That's why these athletes that are coming up need this kind of support. All my friends were either getting married or they had really good jobs or were travelling overseas. You must weigh that up as well. They had houses, they bought houses and here I was getting up to 20, 21 years old going, 'What do I have? What do I want?' I never questioned not playing though. I always thought that I would still play and I guess I probably didn't feel like I was getting what I needed out of it at the time."

Tracey admitted that she was always looking to challenge herself, whether it was with hockey or away from the field of play.

"I used to train and then I went and trained with some of the men's teams, imagine that," she said with a laugh. "We had Walshy (Terry Walsh) and Charlie (Ric Charlesworth) there, as well as David Bell, who were all still playing at the time, and I wanted to train with the men's team, just to be better and learn different things. Brian got wind of it and told me I was not to do that. So, I used to have to have sneak training with them. I trained with South Perth (now WASPs) for a little bit. Frank Murray was the coach at the time, which was great. They had people like David Wansborough in the team and people like that, and it might have been only little pieces here and there I picked up, but to have that opportunity was fantastic. The fact that I had to sneak around and do that stuff to get better really pissed me off. So, in the end I said, 'you know what? I don't want to be here.'"

"I know I wasn't the fittest or the fastest, but I think I understood the game and I was skilful enough, I just wanted to soak up more. I rang Ric Charlesworth up and said, 'Can you come down and do a session with me?' at 17. I rang David Bell up and said, 'Can we do a tackling session?' I rate my tackling during the time I played for Australia very highly. It's not the same now. There's not the same importance placed on it because it is a totally different game, but I was proud to say the player I was marking on that day might have got around me once in the whole game, if that. That's how I looked at that type of skill, and so I was that type of person. I wasn't egotistical enough or shy enough to not do that and I thought, 'I'm in WA, I'm where all these legends are that I've looked up to and watched on the television forever, why wouldn't I ring them up and talk to them about hockey, and go to Dibsy's [David Bell's] house for drinks and chat to him about hockey or Michael Nobbs?' These were fantastic, wonderful legends of our game. I was just a sponge and wanted to talk to them about it and talk about different things about the game. You can learn so much. I did that while I was there whenever I could. I just loved that."

Tracey was selected and came back to Perth to prepare for the Olympic Games, and she would be part of the trio of young players joined by Rechelle Hawkes and Sally Carbon. She was the youngest in the squad.

Debbie Bowman

Debbie was born on 4 July 1963 in Southport, Queensland, and grew up in Musgrave Hill on the Gold Coast.

Her journey in hockey was far from normal, as she explained. "My street played, and we didn't live far from the Hockey Centre, just a street away. My father became interested because of my interest, and he picked up a set of hockey sticks and took it to the school and it went from there."

Although it was not quite as easy or straightforward for Bowman's father. For a start, girls at the school did not play hockey at that time.

"Women couldn't play hockey. It was a very male-dominated sport," Bowman recalled. "There was a lot of negativity, [enough] for Dad to say, 'we want hockey in the school, and we don't want it to be predominantly the boys playing it, we want the girls to play'. He had a lot of brick walls put up because the stigma back then was [that] it was a boys' sport."

"My Dad ended up coaching us. He was high up in the rugby league. Valleys [Fortitude Valley Diehards] was an A-Grade rugby league side and there was surf lifesaving too that he was into, and his picture is still up in the Main Beach Surf Lifesaving club today with his crew. He was a very active father in sport. I was very fortunate I inherited my Dad's big heart, and I was a bit like Phar Lap, and anything I did in the sporting arena, be it running, hockey or swimming, it was easy for me. So, through school I did everything until Mum and Dad said, 'you are going to have to cut something. You're running and swimming at a high level you need to go with what your passion is.'"

"I had other siblings, so it was not all about me. I had an older sister, 16 months older than me, and another sister five years younger, all playing the sport of hockey, so it was easier to go to the hockey field in those days. Back then, all the games were on the same day, so it was just one day. It's not like that anymore. "

"Mum was in the administration side, Dad was in the coaching and running the ground, and both my parents were on the club board, so it was easier for me to opt out of swimming and running, which I both loved. Swimming I looked at that and thought, honestly, to follow that black line is just going to do my head in! When it came to running, I enjoyed running and it was something Dad and I did together, but I enjoyed being part of a team, and it was easier for Mum and Dad to have us all go to one place rather than here and there, and in athletics you had to go to Brisbane, so that was out."

"Although I loved running. Mum and Dad had issues when I came home from school at a very young age. Mum would say, 'you need to do your homework', and Dad would say, 'Why don't you come for a 10 km run?' You can guess what I chose. I always went against what was my Mum's ideal pathway, or what she would have liked me to do. Running was a passion, and something I did with my Dad. So, I never had any issues with training when I did all my Olympics. It was just good to run, and so enjoyable."

Despite starting the game at a very young age, just when it appeared everything was going along smoothly, Bowman received a severe jolt which she has never forgotten. "I had a hockey stick in my hand at four and played in games at seven in under 8s, and made my debut for the Queensland senior side at 16. Of course, back then we were on grass and not a synthetic surface. I did miss a senior selection when I was 16. As I remember it, someone said that I had put on weight and I wasn't as fast, and I went 'oooh, ouch! Take that dagger out of my heart.' That was my turnaround, the time when I realised that I had to put in a little more than I was currently doing, and not rely on what came naturally. I was hairdressing at the time and eating the wrong food. So, that was a good wake up call for me to miss out on selection."

While many dream of representing their country, for Bowman it was not something that she says that she thought about, and the Olympic Games was never in her thoughts.

"If it came along, that would be great, but I never really focused on it," she explained. "Even when the Olympic Games came around, and I know this sounds awful, but it was never ever a goal. I have always worked and be it my work life or my personal life, I have always believed if you do the right processes every day it will come naturally. People talk about goals, long- term, short-term, but that was never me. Do whatever I am doing to my fullest, and the rest will naturally happen, that is what I have always believed."

Sharon Buchanan

Sharon was born in Busselton on 12 March 1963. It is a coastal town approximately 200 km southwest of Perth in Western Australia. She would start playing hockey in the town but at the age of around 13, she moved to Perth.

"I had an older brother, and we moved because he finished school, but the move was also for my hockey. Just my Mum, my brother and I made the move."

"The first club I played for in Perth was Fremantle. I went there because a very good friend of ours from Busselton was coaching – John Leece – Terry Leece's son who had also played for Australia, so he was my mentor and coach. I had him coach me at Fremantle, and I was there for three years before I moved to West Grads as it was, now known as Westside Wolves."

As for aspiring to play for Australia, Buchanan admits that it never really entered her mind. "In my day, I didn't even know there was an Australian team, it was a very different scenario. I did know there was a team, as a few of the older ladies from Busselton had made it to play for Australia, so I was aware there was a national team, but didn't know much about it. I just loved playing, and enjoyed training and working hard, and getting better. I think it just went from there."

Buchanan was selected for the Australian squad following the National Championships in 1979 and was then selected to go to the Moscow Olympics at the age of 17. Despite no doubt having many years of her hockey career ahead of her, she admitted that the disappointment of not attending the 1980 Olympic Games made her more determined.

"Not having had that opportunity, and we had to qualify. For me, I just wanted to play for Australia. I wanted to put on my uniform and play for my country. I just wanted to get out there and be amongst it!"

She would be a part of the team that made Australia's first Olympic Games appearance in 1984, but it was not a tournament that many would remember fondly.

"The Dutch were favourites in '84. We should have come home with a medal. Elspeth broke her thumb on the way there, so we lost our main full back, which was a blow, and we were up and down with our performances. It was a round-robin competition back then. In the last games, we played the Dutch and could have won a gold medal had we beaten them by two goals or won silver if we had beaten them by one or drawn, so it was all very complicated. However, if we lost by two, which we did, we had to go into a shoot-out with the Americans straight after our game. It was all a bit unusual. As history shows, we missed out."

Those two disappointments meant that Buchanan was determined to make sure that in '88 the team fulfilled their potential. "We had the potential to be successful and heading into '88 there was a definite shift in focus, and I think we found a belief that we could be successful."

Lee Capes

Lee Capes was born on 3 October 1961. Her mother and her aunt had both played hockey for Australia, so you would have assumed that Lee would automatically gravitate to the sport, but that was not the case.

"I wanted to go to Wimbledon as a tennis player. I watched Evonne Goolagong, and I remember staying up and watching her play and win the final. So that was what I wanted to be. That was my aspiration. Then I took tennis lessons, and I was terrible!" She laughs at the memory.

Her transition to hockey was far from normal but was heavily influenced by her mother. "My Mum played hockey for Australia, and my auntie also played for Australia. When I was about nine, there was no junior hockey in those days, but Mum pulled together a team of young ones, mainly the daughters of people who were still playing at the club, and Mum created this team, and we played in the ladies' competition."

Capes would however show talent in several sports, and she was attracting attention as a high jumper in athletics.

"Athletics was what I did in summer, hockey was what I did in winter," she explained. I was a State high jumper and I used to train with Vanessa Ward – she was Vanessa Brown then– she went to the '84 and '88 Olympics and was awesome. Her Dad was my coach, and I got to about age 15 or 16, and athletics wanted me to do stuff in the off-season. Hockey wanted the same, so I had to make a choice. I knew I had the potential to be better at hockey than I did as a high jumper, and I knew I would never be as good as Vanessa, so I chose hockey."

Despite her hockey genes, Capes' path to the top was not a smooth one.

"I played under-16s for Tassie when I was 11, because we lived in Tasmania for a couple of years. Then at 15 I played for Western Australia because we had moved back to Perth. I played under-19s for a couple of years, but I just couldn't crack the senior WA side because basically the national team had the WA forward line: Colleen Pearce, Marion Bell, Janice Bell, Gail Smith and Susie Wood. They were all from WA, so for four or five years I could not get in the State team."

Then I met Michael (Australian men's player Michael Nobbs), who was playing for Australia and coaching an opposition women's team. One day I said to him, 'look I may as well give up there's no point. I can't break into this

State team because I am not an Australian player.' Over the summer, he said, 'Why don't we work on what you are good at, so that you get better at it?'"

"I was fast, and I knew where the goals were, and so he said, 'Ok I will teach you two or three skills for your speed'. I said, 'yeah, but the coaches keep telling me I am not a good tackler'. He said, 'who cares, you don't get picked for what you are bad at, you get picked for what you are good at. So, let's take what you are good at and make you really good at it!'"

"I had only played my first senior State team game at 23, so that gap from 19-23 can either make or break you, and especially knowing that my sister who was a defender, and five years younger than me, got picked in the State senior team as a 17-year-old, I would watch the State Championships, and she was playing, and I couldn't get in the side! But then we both made the Australian team together, and that was in '84."

Her hard work and never giving up paid dividends when eight spots at the Australian Institute of Sport were up for grabs after the 1984 Olympic Games.

"Thank God I got one of those. I knew I had to make the Australian team to stay in the State team when they all came back. Fortunately, I made the Australian team straight away when I was in the AIS. I knew then that being selected for Seoul was a possibility."

Michelle Capes

Michelle was also born on 3 October, but five years after older sister Lee in 1966. You would assume that she had little choice but to play hockey when growing up as her sister was playing and being coached by their Mum.

"Being the youngest child of four, I got dragged along to Mum's and my sisters' games and yeah, I just guess I had no choice really," she admits, laughing at the memory. "Although, when I was about 15, I gave up hockey and my mother was horrified. I wanted to go and play netball with my friends and she's like, 'Oh my God!' She was dying, because that was on a Saturday morning, and then on the Saturday afternoon I wanted to go to the football with my Dad. I used to go to the East Fremantle games with my Dad and play netball with my friends on a Saturday morning. She said she was OK with it, but I knew she wasn't. That was just for one year and then I went, 'Okay, back to hockey!'"

Incredibly, growing up there was another member of the team headed to Seoul that was good friends with Michelle and Lee, and that was Jackie Pereira.

"We all did Little Athletics and there were about five or six families that ended up being good friends from the Melville Little Athletics Centre, and that's how we all met. We used to have family barbecues and all sorts of things. That was before Jackie even started playing hockey. The families would always go away together, and I've been friends with Jackie as far back as I can remember. She started playing hockey for Willetton, and she was playing down the grades, like fourth or fifth grade, and my Mum said to her, 'come to Fremantle and play with Michelle'. So, she started off there and I think she was one year in third and second grade and then back up into first grade, and then the State teams. So, she never did under-16s or anything like that because she started later. I think her first State teams were under-19s and then under-21s and then within two or three years, she was in the senior State teams and then the national team."

"We all didn't make it until '84. I made it in '83, just out of pure luck. They were missing a defender, so I was just lucky enough to get a spot. But we all made it in '84 when the regular players were away. None of them competed at the Nationals, because they must've been away, so we all broke into the State side. After the '84 Olympics, a lot of them retired so we all just stayed in it, and it was a new group coming through together."

"As I said, I played Nationals in '83 and then Jackie and myself were accepted into the AIS in '84. A lot of the older ones weren't. It was almost a regeneration thing."

Despite her progress in the game, like many, Michelle Capes confessed that she too had not really considered going to the Olympic Games as a hockey player.

"As a kid, I always watched the Olympics, and thought, 'oh wow, wouldn't that be cool', but not necessarily the hockey. It was all the sports really, and then I guess it was just all a progression – right age, right time, as well as a little bit of luck, because after '84, as I said, there were a number of retirements, so I think we were all quite lucky to be there at the right time."

Sally Carbon

Sally Carbon was another Western Australian selected for Seoul. Born in Perth on 14 April 1967, she was one of the youngest in the side.

Like so many players, she became involved due to her mother's influence. "My Mum played, so we did the old run around on the sideline at training and at the game, and I think my first game was me simply playing, probably quite young, about eight or nine years old, and Mum's playing First or Second Division at that time for Floreat, and one day they were one player short, so they literally threw a hockey stick at me and I ran on and played."

Once again, like some of her colleagues, for Sally there was no aspiration to play hockey for Australia, but she knew that she did want to wear the national colours.

"I was actually quite an able sportsperson. I was asked to go into the Australian ballet. I was asked to move to Germany when I was young as a gymnast. I represented Western Australia in athletics. I played softball a little bit later on, and I was a pretty good swimmer, I probably could've been a swimmer as well. I just badly wanted to play sport all the time. I used to come home from primary school, I walked home every day, I would put my bag down on the side of an oval and I would run 200m. I'd do that every day and I was visualising Australia written across the back of my tracksuit. So, I definitely wanted to represent Australia, but the sport was secondary to me, it didn't really matter which sport it was."

Having made her debut in October 1987 on the eve of an Olympic Games, you would have expected Carbon to have had one eye on Olympic selection, but she revealed that she honestly did not really give it a thought.

"No, I didn't think [about it]. The beauty of that time, for someone who now is just a ridiculously heavy thinker, I think the reason why I was so successful early on is because I didn't think. After that Seoul competition, we had the Bicentennial Tournament in Perth which was against the Dutch. Now I didn't know the power of the Dutch. I knew the pitch about how good they were , but I didn't have that tarnished view that the Dutch were much better than us. So, I also played in that Bicentennial Tournament against the Dutch and I absolutely killed it, and I can remember I probably got the best goal of my entire career six months into my career."

"Absolute freedom rather than thinking about whether I was going to get in the Olympic team, or the Dutch are so good, or Australia's ranking, or getting paid to play. You know, all the things that happen to you later in life. I just played with complete freedom."

Elspeth Denning

Elspeth Denning, who became the first woman to play 100 games for Australia in Seoul, was born in Kenya on 19 June, 1956. At the age of six, her family moved to South Africa and when she was 19, they moved to Australia.

"It was hard for my Mum and Dad as there were six of us and the first two didn't want to go. I didn't want to go, but I knew that I had to go, as I was quite scared of not being with my family. My second sister, Pam, had a long-term boyfriend and I thought she was going to jump off the boat when we left," Elspeth explained. "Dad gave us a choice whether we wanted to come by boat or plane. We all said 'boat', as it would take longer to get there. I thought Pam was going to run, but she came, got the first job she could, saved up her money and in six months she was back. She did end up coming back to Australia in the 1980s."

Australia in the 1970s was very different to the South Africa they left behind. Elspeth admitted that she was very wary of the new life that awaited her. "Honestly, I had come from South Africa to Australia, and I was a bit fearful about travelling because we had come from a country where there was apartheid, and then there was Russia and America constantly arguing. We had no TV in South Africa, so we were quite sheltered from the world. I had never watched TV until I came to Australia."

Having made her debut for Australia in 1979, and being selected for the 1980 Moscow Olympic Games, Elspeth was one of those who missed out when Australia boycotted the Games. Then in 1984, she was selected for the Los Angeles Olympic Games, only to get injured in one of the warm-up games. So, by 1988, she was chomping at the bit to get on the pitch and play following her third Olympic selection.

"Come '88, I just wanted to get on the field. I knew once I stepped on the field, I was an Olympian, and no one could ever take it away from me. Brian was very good in that he protected me a lot to make sure that I did make the field. I stopped running out at corners and he had me stand on the post, which thinking back now was probably worse, but I felt a bit safer there. Once I stepped on the field, I was OK."

"All the media were making a big thing of it saying, 'What are you going to do if you don't play?' I remember saying, 'I will be so angry if I don't play'."

"This time around, Tracey Belbin broke her thumb, and they went to great lengths to have her still play, which I will be honest made me a bit angry, because I felt that they could have done the same for me in Los Angeles."

Having been selected for two Olympic Games, some may have wondered if the opportunity was going to pass them by, but not Elspeth. As forthright as ever, she admitted, "I was confident I would make the team. I always knew I would be in the team, as long as something didn't happen. I know that sounds terrible, but the way we had been playing, I was confident."

Prior to the Games, she told the press: "Had I played in LA, I would not have felt disappointed – even though there was no medal won there. This time I know I want to do it and we'll definitely get a medal. We won't make the mistake of wanting gold from our first game. We'll just take each game as it comes and aim to make the finals." Then in a quote for ages, she stated: "I don't care what we win in Seoul. It can be anything as long as it is not nothing."

She concluded by revealing her plans once the Olympics were over. "I come home, retire, never run again, and have kids. There is no point going on. I'm 30, that wouldn't be so bad for the blokes, but not me. I hate the training and the running. I have had so much hockey now that it's time to get out."

Loretta Dorman

Loretta Dorman was born on 23 July 1963 and spent her early years in the Australian Capital Territory where she attended St Clare's High School.

She came from a fairly large family in which Australian rules football was very much the focus. It was not until just before her teenage years that she first picked up a hockey stick.

"I started when I was 12. I don't know, girls never really got into organised sports too much back then. I wanted to play some sport and I thought, 'well, all right I'll try netball', but didn't really like having to stop at the lines all the time, and then one of my sisters, my older sister, was playing hockey, so I went down and had a bit of a run around with her at a practice match and their coach, who was an English lady said, 'oh she looks like she could be okay', and that's how it all started really. I just liked it from the word go."

There were no athlete pathways in those days, and as Loretta admitted, no one really gave her any feedback on her performances.

"I was in the ACT, so it was a pretty small environment in terms of the competition that was there. I know that the coach that I had was amazing, an English coach who played lots of different styles. We didn't play a traditional Australian style even with our club team."

"Pat Pyne was her name, she was from England, and, as I said, she was an amazing coach. I was very, very lucky to have fallen into her hands because she gave me so much guidance and just let things flow. She was just an amazing mentor. I think she was the one who said that I should just go along to a trial. I went along to a trial, and I guess it just snowballed from there. But if she hadn't told me to go, I doubt I would have gone."

From that trial, Loretta continued on a path to the national team, although she admitted that it was never an ambition to play for Australia.

"I didn't really aspire to be an Australian player. I didn't really think about it probably until I was about 18 or so, and even then, it was a case of maybe that you would get in or whatever that looked like." She revealed that she didn't even consider the possibility of joining the Institute of Sport program."

"The institute didn't start until I was 20, so even then it wasn't something I really thought about. I just loved playing; I loved training. I used to train over on the oval with my brothers. We didn't have turf back then when I started playing. We used to play footy in winter and hockey and cricket and other sports in summer, that was just the way it went. I played softball in summer and hockey in winter."

"In '84 when the Institute started in Perth, I went over there on a scholarship and we played a lot of games against the Australian squad at that time, and I was a bit of a bolter and got into the team from nowhere really."

Maree Fish

Maree Fish was born in Tasmania on 23 January 1963. She was the only member of the squad to come from the 'Apple Isle'. She started playing hockey at primary school in Hobart.

"My first foray into hockey was in grade 5 at Lindisfarne Primary School in Hobart. I had a go at running around the field but never found a spot I liked. In grade 6, I tried netball but came back to hockey at Rose Bay High in year 7," Maree remembered. "My sister Lyn, who was a goalkeeper playing A Grade with the Hobart-based Wellington Hockey Club, coached the team, so I followed in her footsteps and played in-goal. Two years later, I was selected into my first Tasmanian team, and travelled to Geelong to play in the under-16 national carnival."

"I went on to represent Tasmania in under-19, under-21 and indoor teams, and in 1983 made the senior State team. I joined Graduates Ladies Hockey club and was part of I think it was two premiership teams."

Even though Fish's sister was lost to the game, she had a huge influence on Maree, possibly without ever realising it. "I used to go and stand behind her when she was playing, and her coach at the time used to call me 'little Fishy'. She was Lynne Fish, and I was 'little Fishy' standing behind the goals. If she hadn't coached the school team, I am not sure what I would have done. I have never really thought about it. That was how I learned because that was how

I saw the game then, from the back of the goal. Had I been standing on the halfway line, I would have had a completely different view."

While gaining State selection at a young age was a good thing, there were downsides. However, like so many children, Maree's parents were supportive. "I remember Mum and Dad driving me up to Burnie or Devonport, or wherever it was for training, and you would drive up there and train for two or three hours and then you would drive back," Maree recalled. "Very early on, my identity was sport. I didn't really do my teenage years until I was 30-odd. My identity was as an athlete, and all those normal things that you do as a teenager, I really didn't do that because I was forever playing hockey, as I was already identified as a decent player, and that is what I did."

As a goalkeeper, a position with limited opportunities, Maree's journey was far from plain sailing.

"When I was at college, there was a club team there, but I never played for them. I am not sure how it happened but the coach of one of the under-16 teams, a lady by the name of Christine Bennett coached the team, I think it may have been the first year when I was picked in the Tasmanian under-16 team, she went around the group and said to us, 'What are your goals in hockey?' Apparently, straight away I said I was going to play for Australia. That lady, Christine Bennett, played for Graduates Ladies Hockey club, and it was this select group of top-notch players. I started playing at that club, and the incumbent goalkeeper stopped playing to let me play because they could see what was happening. I turned 18 when I was playing for them, and we won a grand final. I was behind six or seven State players and a couple of Australian players, so that group were huge for me. I was very, very shy when I was at school and they got a little of that out of me, and subsequently all the travel did that as well."

"It got to a stage where I had to leave that club because I was standing there doing nothing, and that's not good when you want to play for Australia. So, I left and went to the bottom club which caused a bit of an uproar, and they said they were not going to clear me to play. That was unfortunate, and sadly my hockey in Hobart and Tasmania in a way ended on a sour note."

Maree made her Australian debut in 1985 and admitted that she had one eye on winning a place at the Olympic Games in 1988.

"I had one eye on the Olympics absolutely, yes. I remember watching the '84 Olympics and Penny Gray (Dundaben), who has since passed away, was from Tasmania. She was at that Olympics and they came fourth, and a lot of them retired after that and so there were a lot of new faces in '85. Those new faces made up a large part of the core group in '88, and I think that is why we were such a close group, and stayed together, because we pretty much had three-and-a-half years together. I think that was a really important part of it."

"I think making the squad, or making the team, it probably wasn't until we got there and we played our first game that it sunk in. It wasn't until we started that first game that you could relax, because if you were injured before that game, you were sent home and replaced. So, until the competition started, it was not real, and I think a few of us had that in the back of our minds."

Rechelle Hawkes

Rechelle Hawkes was born in Albany, Western Australia on 30 May 1967. Albany is a country town 418 km southeast of Perth. It was founded on 26 December 1826 as a military outpost of New South Wales, with its main purpose being to forestall French ambitions in the region.

Like many, Rechelle's hockey influence came from her mother. "We travelled a lot, we were living in country towns because Dad was a policeman, so we basically moved around every two or three years, and I got into it because, obviously, regional sport was quite strong, and my Mum played hockey herself. So, she was the one that started the Gym Association in Wundowie when I was six years of age and I basically got into it from there."

"I played every sport imaginable when I was living in the regional towns, so that was basketball, softball, tennis, squash, hockey, and I did athletics as well. So, I was very keen on playing sport, it didn't matter what it was. I tried my hand at basketball and tennis but then, when we eventually moved to the city, hockey became the chosen sport because I had to give up the others. So, probably from around the age of I guess about 10 I started to really think about whether I could represent the State, and then go on and represent my country. It was probably from around the age of 10 [that] my mind started wondering whether I could represent my country or not."

Hawkes made her debut against West Germany in 1985 at the age of 18.

"It was a real surprise to me, and it came out of the blue because I hadn't made the Western Australian senior side yet," Hawkes admitted. "So, I actually made the Australian team before I represented WA. It was very much a surprise to me, because obviously there's that pathway that you normally take doing the State teams and then you get into a senior State team and then hopefully, if you're good enough, you then progress into the Australian team. So, it was a little bit of a different pathway for me."

"It was very difficult to get into the Western Australian side at that time. I think in Seoul, there were seven Western Australians in that team from memory. Well eight, as Lorraine Hillas was playing for WA but she came from Queensland. It was still about seven or eight, something like that. So that is a huge number of Australian representative players coming from the one State. I mean it's unheard of these days. You never get that many players from one State representing Australia."

Hawkes had ambitions to play at the highest level and go to an Olympic Games, but she had a level head on her young shoulders and knew that anything can happen, good or bad.

"I think initially when I was first selected, I didn't really know what path I was going to take, because you go into, a national program at the age of 18, and there's a lot of senior players there that have been around a long time and you're not quite sure of how you're going to go. How you're going to fit in. Whether you're going to be good enough. I guess I was a bit uncertain about whether I could make Seoul in 1988. So, it was just a case of knuckling down and getting on with it, and training as hard as I could and seeing what would happen in the future. It panned out that I did make it, but it wasn't an easy selection, I don't think. I certainly wasn't one that would've been at the top of the list to be picked for the Seoul Olympic Games, but it was a pathway for me, and the development and the continual improvement was what it was all about. So, I feel very fortunate to have gone in '88, but that then helped pave the way for future Olympic Games."

Lorraine Hillas

Lorraine Hillas was born in Brisbane on 11 December 1961.

At the age of seven, her father was transferred to Cairns in Far North Queensland with his job. "It was a great place to grow up," Lorraine said. "You could ride your bike to training and ride home."

Growing up, Lorraine was into basketball and swimming, and her involvement in hockey came out of the blue. As she remembered it, "a hockey team was two players short and so they asked my sister Kerry and I to play. I think I was in grade six at the time." They would then play for Saints in Cairns.

After nine years, it was time to return to Brisbane and the two sisters played for Valleys in Division Two of the Brisbane competition. It was during one of these games that the two sisters were spotted and invited to join the St Andrews Ladies Hockey club. "They must have been desperate," Lorraine said, and admitted that basketball was still her first love at that time.

"I was lucky to have a great coach, Jan Hadfield and then Jim Quaite, both were amazing. They were the reason I got anywhere in the game."

"I was in Brisbane for two years and made the State squad and then the Australian squad. I didn't think about playing for Australia, I just went with the flow," she admitted. "Even on my first trip away with the Queensland side, I didn't even think of playing for Australia. I just went along for the ride. I had injured my calf and one of my teammates said, 'you have a good chance of making the Australian squad'. That was probably the first time I ever thought about it."

Lorraine was one of the first intake at the AIS in Perth in 1984. "I thought I was going for a year, but it ended up being nine years!"

Both Lorraine and her sister Kerry would go on and play for Australia. However, according to Lorraine, "getting there was easier than staying there!"

Kathleen Partridge

Kath Partridge was born in Sydney on 7 December 1963, but grew up in Armidale, New South Wales. Armidale is a city in the Northern Tablelands approximately halfway between Sydney and Brisbane.

She was educated at O'Connor Catholic College from 1976 to 1981, and while at the school Kath was involved in playing and coaching hockey. However, her introduction to the sport came about by accident.

When she was around the age of 15, she was supposed to have a piano lesson on a Saturday afternoon but one week it was cancelled. She decided to stroll down to Harris Park and watch two of her friends from school play hockey.

The regular goalkeeper did not turn up and so her friends worked hard to convince Kath to go in goal. The word is that she was none too keen initially, but eventually succumbed to their pleas. As they say, from that day on the rest is history.

Team coach Arthur Adams was impressed by what he saw and was looking for a goalkeeper for the under-16 representative team that he also coached. So, Kath was picked for her first representative team after a handful of games in 1979.

She excelled and was selected for the New England under-19 team to compete at the New South Wales Championships, but an injury in an early game meant that the selectors missed out on seeing the talent she had.

In 1982, at the age of 18 and committed to her university studies, she was considering giving up the game, but once again her friends had a lasting impact. Her university friends convinced her that they needed her in goal for the Intervarsity Championships. Kath was selected for the All-Australian Intervarsity team.

Soon after, she was in Newcastle representing New England in the First Division of the State Championships. With New England fielding an understrength team, Kath came under the spotlight as she repelled attack after attack and pulled off many saves. Her reward was selection for the New

South Wales team to play in the National Championships in Adelaide.

Once again, she had an outstanding tournament, and following the event was named in the Australian squad for 1982.

Kath's dream of playing for Australia apparently started following that first representative selection. According to her brother Greg, "she was extremely driven". She was also helped by her Dad who spent hours in the backyard coaching her.

While at the University of New England and playing for the Checkmates club, Kath showed her commitment, dedication and discipline to succeed in all areas of her life, even at such a young age.

She put a routine in place that saw her go swimming, running or weight training prior to her studies each morning. In the afternoon, she would kick or stop up to 300 balls fired at her by a machine purchased by the New England Hockey Association specifically for training goalkeepers.

When the AIS opened its hockey centre in Perth in 1984, Kath was one of the first 16 players awarded a full-time scholarship. That same year she went on her first overseas tour to Europe with the AIS. A year later, she made her debut for Australia when England and Korea came to visit in 1985.

Kath played in the World Cup in 1986 and once in the Australian setup, she continued to strive to be the best that she could be. Yet being the private person that she was, she never shared her goals or ambitions with anyone. They were for her to know and to achieve.

She is the only person from Armidale who has ever won a gold medal at the Olympic Games.

Jackie Pereira

Jackie Pereira was born in the Perth suburb of Subiaco on 29 October 1964.

"I started playing when I was about ten because I was the youngest of four children, and they all started playing hockey before me," Pereira remembered. "So, in the winter we played hockey, and in the summer we played basketball in the Willetton Sports Club. That was how it all started for me."

"I guess with hockey I wasn't a very skilful player, but I seemed to be able to find the goals, which was always very handy," was her modest assessment of her ability. No doubt as a result of that personal assessment, she confirmed that she harboured no dreams of representing Australia.

"I had no dreams initially, as it was so far from the concept that I would ever play for Australia. Although Mum and Dad always said that pretty much as soon as I was born, I always had some kind of ball in my hand. So, I did enjoy sports of any kind, and I did Little Athletics as well. Any sport that was going on, I wanted to be a part of it."

Pereira was selected for Western Australia as a teenager in 1983, and then was offered a place at the Australian Institute of Sport in 1984. That was when she started to believe that playing at the Olympic Games may be a possibility.

"When in 1984 I was one of the inaugural members of the AIS in Perth, and obviously that year there was the Los Angeles Olympics, and some of the AIS students were in the Olympic team, [so] that made me realise that maybe one day I could play for Australia," she revealed.

She made her debut in 1986 at the Esanda International competition in Sydney, a moment she clearly remembers.

"When I was first picked for the national team in 1986, I actually heard on the radio before I was told in person. So that was quite funny. One of the team rang me and said that things had somehow got mixed up and for some reason they were unable to ring me at home. Of course, back then it was only home phones and not mobile phones."

Looking back on the mood in the squad leading up to the Seoul Olympics, Pereira believed that there was a shift about two years out, and again six months out from the Games with a victory over the Dutch.

"I think we were all aware that they could have won the gold medal in '84, but as the game went on, they could have won the silver and then the bronze, and then it went down to the penalty shoot-out. They ended up fourth, and of course we all knew about that, but it wasn't until around 1986 when we knew the Dutch were always the number one team in the world, and every time we played them, we thought that they were the number one team in the world. So, in the back of our minds, even though we tried really hard against them, I think we always felt they can't be beaten."

"Then we had a tournament in Perth at the start of 1988, and we actually won that tournament. After beating the Dutch at that, we had the belief that we could beat them, and every tournament after that we played knowing that we could beat this team, and I think from that came the belief that we could win a medal."

In the lead-up to the Games, one newspaper wrote: "*Pereira is a mouse-like centre striker who sits just off the action until a crumb drops. Then she moves with unerring swiftness and accuracy. Goal to Australia.*"

It was not a bad way to be perceived, and Australia was hoping that she could live up to that reputation.

She subsequently became the first Australian to score 100 goals in international hockey, with her 175 matches producing a total of 109 goals for her country.

Sandy Pisani

Sandy Pisani was born in Adelaide, South Australia on 23 January 1959. Growing up with three brothers would have a huge impact on her, although she probably did not realise it at the time.

She was highly competitive, and according to some, "brutal" on the pitch. This was her competitive nature manifesting itself in a physicality that had been necessary when playing with her brothers. When she walked onto the pitch, she took no prisoners.

Sandy attended Campbelltown High School where she was fortunate to be taught by Volleyball Australia Hall of Famer Sue Dansie, who encouraged her in her sporting pursuits.

She joined Burnside Hockey Club as a junior after encouragement from her friend Sharon Stewart, who played for Heathpool.

On joining Burnside, Sandy became friends with Susie Watkins and Sally Nobbs. The three would become known as "the three S's", and away from hockey would spend many a weekend at Port Gawler beach bodysurfing and sunbathing.

"Everything she did in life, Sandy gave 100%. She couldn't give less, that was what people loved about her," Susie Watkins recalled. "She played hard, but hard and fair. She was like an Amazon; she had a real presence."

According to all who knew her, Sandy stood out from a young age and progressed through the South Australian junior sides. During those formative years, she was not just known for her competitiveness, but also her endurance and the ability to outrun people. She also had a turn of pace that gave her a few yards on her opponents.

Bruce Bowley was her first coach and he recognised her talent. As legend has it, he said, "she could run like a gazelle, and she had an eye like a dead fish." This old expression meant that she never took her eye off the ball, which helps to explain what many have described as "her extraordinary hand-to-eye co-ordination".

According to Susie Watkins, "she never thought about playing for Australia, that was something that evolved. She was so competitive that once she was playing for the State, obviously the next goal was to play for Australia. I think it was only then that she started to think about playing for her country."

"In those days it was very hard to be selected from South Australia. Western Australia, Queensland and New South Wales were the dominant hockey States. South Australia was improving. But once she was in the side, she was in. She always had goals in everything she did, and she was someone who always achieved those goals."

In 1985, Sandy became the first South Australian to captain the Australian women's hockey team.

"When you consider how hard it was to be a South Australian and make the team, to be awarded the captaincy of the side was something that she was incredibly proud of," Susie shared. "She saw it as a huge honour and it made her very happy. She was so highly regarded and respected by everyone. She was an ideal choice."

Sandy won the State's best and fairest award in both 1985 and 1992.

Everyone agrees that she was a real character. She had the ability to light up a room, she loved a laugh and a drink, and she was known to have strong opinions, but like so many in the team, she knew when to switch on for the game.

Sandy went on to become a selector for the Australian team and held that role when the Australian women's hockey team won gold at the 1996 and 2000 Olympic Games.

"She was such a great person who was successful at whatever she did because she always gave 100%," Susie concluded. "But it was the love of her family that was always most important to her."

Kim Small

Kim Small was born on 13 April 1965 and started playing hockey in the country town of Tamworth around the age of 10.

"Some school mates invited me along to training one afternoon," she recalled, adding that "my longest, and 'bestest' friend Vicki Cox was the instigator of all of that, and that was how I got started."

"I then went on and played with a high school team in the A-Grade comp, and then when I left school I changed to, funnily enough, the Olympians club in Tamworth."

Clearly Kim not only took to the game, but also had a talent for it as she was selected for the State under-19 team in 1984 and "was then invited to be on the Australian Institute of Sport's touring side in '84 and the Institute in Perth in '85 and '86."

As she explained, things were very different back then. "I played New South Wales under-19s, we didn't have the progression that they have these days when it starts in your early teens."

As for ambition, like many of her gold-medal winning teammates, Kim played the game first and foremost because she loved it.

"I loved the game, and I still play the game. It was a case of the higher the level of competition, the more I liked it. I never had any desire to represent Australia, but I always wanted to play at the highest level of competition possible. I think that was what drove me more than anything else, and still does."

As for the Olympic Games, "that was not really in my mind when I moved to the AIS, it was more about being able to represent Australia. You always wanted to get into the next team, and that progression obviously meant World Cups and Olympic teams, but every time you didn't make a team, you got very disappointed. I had no four or five-year goal in terms of what I wanted to do. I just wanted to play, and at the highest level I could."

Kim remembers the selection process and admitted that she was not confident she would make the team.

"It was in May in 1988, I do remember that because I was concerned that I wasn't going to make it because I had a broken toe at the tournament. I remember it was a case of your name being called then and there, and announced in front of your peers, I think that was a good thing. Although if you didn't make it, then maybe it might not be such a good thing," she said with a chuckle, before adding, "in fact it was nerve-wracking, as my name was always at the end of the alphabet! It would have been nice if they started at the other end occasionally!"

Liane Tooth

Liane Tooth was born in Sydney on 13 March 1962 and she started playing hockey when she went to high school.

"I went to PLC (Presbyterian Ladies College) in Sydney, or one of the two PLCs in Sydney, and I started I think by seeing a hockey stick in the corner of my elder sister's room, who had played it for one year, and she didn't like it and had moved onto netball. I think my Mum played it when she was at school at PLC, so I just gave it a go and loved it."

It would be fair to say that Liane came from good sporting stock. Her Dad was a former Australian rugby union international and Test captain, Dr Richard Murray 'Dick' Tooth. He was a prominent backline player who made his Test debut against the All Blacks at five-eighth in 1951. He would later captain the Wallabies against the All Blacks.

Some may have expected on the back of her father playing international sport that Tooth would have been pushed to strive for a similar goal, but she said this was never the case.

"I don't know if Mum and Dad had aspirations for that. I don't have any recollections of ever being pushed. Dad was an extremely humble sort of person, and didn't talk too much about his achievements, but certainly I had the support of my parents to play sport. It was just kind of a gradual evolution as I continued to play and enjoyed it and ended up being pretty good at it. I certainly wasn't pushed or shoved into it or anything like that, but definitely supported all the way through."

As for her own ambitions, "it's something that evolved. I'm definitely not one of those people that you speak to that's like, 'I knew when I was eight years old that I wanted to go to the Olympics or play for Australia or whatever'. Probably, to be fair, when I started playing hockey, I probably wasn't even aware that there were State teams and national teams. It was a gradual thing. I think I probably got into club hockey because one of the 'phys-ed' teachers at one of the schools we regularly played against in the private school system played for one of the local North Shore teams in Sydney, and I think it was through that. I kind of got encouraged to come down and try out for an under-16s team. From there, they asked if I'd be interested in coming along and playing there."

"So, I started playing club hockey. I'm just trying to think how old I would've been, probably 15 or something. I started playing grade hockey as well and I eventually got picked in a North Shore under-16 team that went to a State Championship and then in an under-19 North Shore team, and gradually into a senior State team. I got into the under-19 New South Wales squad, I think I was in that team for two years, and at that stage they didn't have under-21s, so it was a leap from under-19s into seniors, and I made the State squad, and then the State team, and I guess it was kind of around then I became more aware that there was a pathway. I remember watching the Australian team play out at the Sydney University hockey pitch and as I watched that I think I became more aware of those stepping-stones, and it became more on my radar then that it was possible. Then the AIS started up in 1984, and I was in the northern intake for that. So, it was kind of just a gradual progression and awareness, I think."

Having been one of the players to suffer the painful loss to the USA in 1984, Tooth felt that the team for '88 had come together well in the subsequent four years and was really well placed with a mix of youth and experience.

"Those that continued to play on after the '84 Olympics, and there was less of the team that played on than I think that retired from it, I think this meant that we had a good strong group of experience mixed with youth. I think we did gel well together. Obviously, we trained a lot together, so we had that opportunity to gel and get to know each other well on and off the field. I think by the time we got to the actual Olympics, we'd beaten the Dutch at the beginning of that year at a tournament in Perth, and I think we really went into the Seoul Olympics believing that we were capable, but that the tide was turning because the Dutch had dominated us so much before then. So, we were reaping the benefits of our expanded training programs, and by the time we got to Seoul, we believed that we could do it."

The team: L-R Front – Sharon Buchanan, Lorraine Hillas, Debbie Bowman, Elspeth Denning, Michelle Capes, Sally Carbon. Back – Yvonne Parsons (Manager), Brian Glencross (Coach) Loretta Dorman, Kathy Partridge, Kim Small, Sandy Pisani, Jackie Pereira, Rechelle Hawkes, Liane Tooth, Lee Capes, Tracey Belbin Peter Freitag, Maree Fish.

Posing with Swedish Tennis star Stefan Edberg, (L - R) Lee Capes, Jackie Pereira, Stefan Edberg, Sharon Buchanan, Michelle Hager and Elspeth Denning.

Village hairdressing: Kim Small, Tracey Belbin, Kathy Partridge and Loretta Dorman.

Getting their groove on, Sharon Buchanan, Liane Tooth, Tracey Belbin, and Loretta Dorman.

The Pig Presentation, which proved more lucky for Australia than South Korea.

Into the gold medal match – The Dutch defeated.

The pocket of loyal Australian fans inside the stadium. (Pic: Kevin Dempster)

A piece of history, a ticket to the gold medal match. (Pic: Kevin Dempster)

The loud and proud South Korean support. (Pic: Kevin Dempster)

United until the very end.

Straight into the action, Maree Fish makes an immediate impact

Congratulations all around, the gold medal is won.

Saluting the crowd. All Smiles post game, (L-R) Tracey
Belbin, Liane Tooth, Debbie Bowman, Elspeth Denning,
Rechelle Hawkes, Sandy Pisani, Lee Capes, Lorraine
Dorman, Sharon Buchanan and Kathy Partridge.

On top of the podium.

The lap of honour, Liane Tooth, Sharon Buchanan, Jackie Pereira, Debbie Bowman, Elspeth Denning, Kim Small, Tracey Belbin, Maree Fish, Loretta Dorman, Lee Capes, Sandy Pisani, and Michelle Capes.

Proudly Australian. Front – Debbie Bowman, Elspeth Denning, Loretta Dorman, and Liane Tooth.
Back – Maree Fish , Brian Miller, Ross Smith (physio), Peter Freitag and Tony Galvin (Doctor).

All Smiles. Front – Kathy Partridge,
Back – Michelle Capes, Sandy Pisani and Jackie Pereira.

Post match drinks – Sally Carbon, Liane Tooth, Loretta
Dorman and Lee Capes

The family connection – Michelle Capes, mum and former international June Harding and sister Lee.

The cartoon in The Sun.

4. LET THE GAMES BEGIN

*"I think we all realised that making the Olympic team could
be harder than winning team gold at the Games itself."*

USA gymnast Aly Raisman

The team arrived in Seoul early to acclimatise to the conditions, although they had played in the trial tournament the year before and so were better prepared than most, as Kim Small explained.

"We had been the year before, so we had had a look at what was happening there, so it wasn't all totally new when we arrived. We settled in really easily, and even though there was the hype about it being an Olympics, I honestly think we weren't caught up in that, and just viewed it as another tournament. I think that was a good thing."

According to Elspeth Denning though, there was a downside to having been to Seoul before. "The food wasn't that great; we didn't like the food. Brian was always on about us eating too much, as we had on one previous trip, and so he took the scales to make sure that we did not eat too much. Whereas on this trip he had us stepping on the scales to make sure that we actually ate enough! We would go into the food hall, walk around and go 'no', then go and eat McDonald's. The best thing about the food hall was looking at all the athletes from other countries."

She went on to explain that even though they were there to compete and try to win a medal, the team never forgot to enjoy their time at the Games. "We had fun. We were serious but we still had fun, and I don't know if they have fun anymore. I think that has gone from the game; it is all too serious today."

"We did everything Brian said. He said that this was going to be a dry trip, and I remember saying to him, 'Brian, don't say that'. 'No, no, it's a dry trip, he insisted.' So, we all had Baileys hidden in our rooms and were drinking at night!"

"Then it was 'no shopping'. I said, 'don't tell them what they can't do'. Of course, once he said this, we all used to sneak out shopping. We would go to Itaewon on our day off. We would sneak back into the Village and put all our packages in the lift and get the security guard to take them to our rooms. We would then walk back up as if we hadn't been anywhere."

"It was great, we loved it. That actually helped to build team spirit. Also, we were very close to the men. We did stupid things like filling condoms with water, and we would bomb everyone. We just had a really good time; we had a really great time. We didn't stress about playing. The more you think about playing, the more you stress about it, and the harder it gets. We knew when it was time to switch on and everyone did."

Prior to the Olympic Games starting, the team had two warm-up games at the Song Nam Olympic Stadium where all the Olympic matches would be played. This was not your traditional hockey stadium, as Sally Carbon explained.

"The thing that was interesting about Song Nam Stadium in Korea was that it had an athletics track, a big oval, so you had your rectangle inside an oval, then an athletics track and then tiered seating all the way around. So, the crowd's a long way away from you, whereas usually playing hockey, your crowd is 1.5m away."

The first of these pre-tournament matches was on 14 September against the USA and resulted in a confidence-boosting 5-0 victory, with a brace from Michelle Capes and single goals from Sally Carbon, Debbie Bowman and Jackie Pereira.

Although that was a positive in terms of a victory with no goals conceded, it was not all good news. In fact, it was almost as if history was repeating itself. Like Elspeth had in 1984, Tracey Belbin picked up a thumb injury.

"We were playing the US and Elspeth had broken her thumb running out from a corner in LA, and as a result she didn't end up playing. It was funny because the US were taking a long corner from the back line, and we'd never done this before, and Elspeth said, 'move right, move right', and I turned around and said, 'normally I'm left and you're right'. Anyway, I was only five yards away and the girl lifted it and hit it straight into my thumb. I dropped my stick and I thought 'oh, it'll be alright, it hurts a lot, it'll be alright'. Then I tried to pick my stick up and I couldn't because my thumb wouldn't work," Tracey recalled.

It looked as if Tracey's Olympic Games were over before they had started. Assistant coach Peter Freitag had that opinion, but as he explained, Brian Glencross had a different view.

"Brian said, 'What do you think we should do?' I said, 'well we get so-and-so in to replace her'. He was not even considering that and said, 'no, no, can't we get something to cover her hand so she can play?' I'm thinking, 'the woman has broken her thumb, there is no way she can play.'"

As Elspeth explained in her usual frank and honest way, "they went to great lengths to have Tracey still play, which I will be honest made me a bit angry, because I felt that they could have done the same for me in Los Angeles. However, saying that, Tony Galvin was the doctor in Seoul, and I remember saying to him, 'try and get her on the field', and he did, which was great for her and the team."

There was still no guarantee that Tracey would play. It was going to take time to see if her injury healed as well as great teamwork, as she explained. "One thing I will say about that time, and I don't say it to a lot of people, but when I talk about Seoul and I talk about teamwork and dedication, I was in the room, and I think we were in rooms of eight or something, and every couple of hours, I had to have my thumb in this magnetic resinous thing. It was a circular thing that was supposed to put rays into it and speed my recovery. Anyway, every couple of hours, my roommates would come and wake me up so that I could continue the treatment. I remember Kath, Loretta and Sharon would wake me up, put this contraption on, [saying] 'now do this, now do that...' You know, all of them really, I have them to thank as well because they all just pulled together and tried to get me right. I was really fortunate to have such really great teammates. Nobody really knows too much about that but... "

Tracey never finished the sentence. The emotion or remembering the support from her teammates after all these years was more than evident.

One day as the team prepared, they were visited by the President of South Korea. Each member of the team was given a large, stuffed-pig toy. To many, it was a strange gift, but in Korean culture, pigs symbolise wealth and luck. This is because historically, only rich Korean people could eat pork. It was a lovely gesture, but one that in time the President may have lived to regret.

It will come as no surprise that Tracey did not play in the second warm-up match on 19 September against Argentina.

If the game against the USA was a satisfying run before the start of Olympic competition, then the one against Argentina would have bolstered the team's confidence even more. The Australians had an emphatic 6-0 victory with Jackie Pereira scoring four and Lee Capes two.

This game was played two days after the official Opening Ceremony of the Seoul Olympics, as unlike more recent hockey tournaments at Olympic Games, in 1988 there were only eight teams contesting the women's event, and they were the best eight teams in the world.

There was no consideration of television revenues at the time or the importance of having teams competing from every region. In that era, it was the best taking on the best.

"You had to be the best at that tournament," was how Sally Carbon put it. "Everything had to go right for you and things like all the rehearsals paid dividends to the extent that all our sticks were labelled in order, nothing was left to chance. So, yes, we had these eight teams and to be perfectly honest, when you're that good, eight out of the 204 nations that play hockey in the world, you've got the absolute cream of the cream, any team's going to win, but it's the team that's most prepared. Plus those little sliding-doors moments that work for you. It is the team that's most prepared that will beat the remaining seven when you're all good together. It's not necessarily the best team, it's the team that's most prepared for that unforeseen situation."

The Opening Ceremony is famous as it was the last one where doves were released. Since 1920, live doves had been released at Olympic Opening Ceremonies as a symbol of peace. For the 1988 Olympics, the birds were trained for a year in preparation for the event where the eyes of the world would be watching. After they were released, the birds were supposed to fly around the stadium in circles until they reached its rim. They were then supposed to fly off in five directions.

However, once released, the birds flew erratically and landed in various parts of the stadium, including on the cauldron where the Olympic flame was to burn for the duration of the Games.

The Olympic flame was carried into the stadium by Kee-chung Sohn, the legendary marathon winner of the 1936 Games, then participating under the name Kitei Son. Then, young sprinter Chun-ae Im passed the flame to the last three torchbearers who lit the cauldron together. Tragically, some of the doves had not left that position and were burnt alive. As can be imagined, there was a worldwide outcry.

Tracey Belbin admitted that when the flame entered the stadium, that was the moment she realised that she was now a part of history. "I actually got to the Opening Ceremony in Seoul, I was standing there and I remember the girl running past me with the flame and going up to the cauldron with the torch, and I thought, 'you know what, if I die tomorrow or something happens, somewhere in some history book, my name is going to be there that I was in the Australian women's hockey team', and this is before the whole tournament even started. I thought, 'that's history and that's what's amazing about this experience and no one can take that away now that I'd been there'. That's what that meant to me."

When the flagbearers of the 160 participating nations entered the stadium, they did so in the order of the Korean alphabet.

This was also an historic moment as it was the last parade to involve East Germany, the Soviet Union, West Germany and Yugoslavia. It was also the only Olympic parade in which South Yemen participated. Within a couple of years, it became the People's Democratic Republic of Yemen.

For Peter Freitag, the Opening Ceremony was an emotional time. "Inside the stadium, the GB team were not that far away from us, and Bernie Cotton, Dave Whittaker and a couple of others who had been involved with me and the Montreal fiasco were there. There was this one photo taken with all the Australians in their gold blazers, and in amongst the Great Britain white blazers is a lone yellow blazer and that was me," he revealed. "I walked across during the Opening Ceremony to talk to them and say, 'isn't it great we are finally here'."

"The Opening Ceremony was absolutely amazing," he continued. "It was emotional. I was desperate to go to an Olympic Games, I was desperate to be an Olympian after Montreal. They lined you up and we were in some sports field near the stadium and when your nation was called you went in through a tunnel under the stand and then you came out of the darkness into the bright sunlight. It was gob-smacking! There were 80,000 people, and they erupted as we walked in and I remember thinking, 'half the world is watching, and I am here, I am an Olympian'. You walk around the stadium, and it was fantastic. I will never forget it. I was so proud of that moment. It was like winning your first cap, no one can ever take it away from you!"

In 1988, the Olympic Games women's hockey tournament was held over ten days and saw the best eight teams in the world split into two pools of four.

Rechelle Hawkes reflected on the tournament with the benefit of hindsight. "If you go back then, there wasn't a whole lot of difference between the teams ranked from one to eight, so there were no easy games. We went in ranked number one or two, but Korea had been playing exceptionally well. You had the Netherlands who were always at the pointy end, and always either ranked number one or two and had won Olympic Games previously. Germany were one of the strongest teams in Europe during the '80s, so there were definitely no easy games. It was a really tough, competitive Olympic campaign and one that, if I reflect on it and looked at some of the games, just some of the goal-scoring opportunities, there was really great work that was done in the semi and finals, and there were some fantastic hockey players. You forget how well the team did play at certain times during that campaign."

In Pool A were the Netherlands, Great Britain, Argentina, and the USA. In Pool B were Canada, West Germany, Australia and hosts South Korea.

"I was concerned about South Korea and Germany because I knew that they would come hard. I wasn't so concerned about Canada," was Elspeth's reaction to the draw.

"At that level, on any given day, any team can win," Liane Tooth explained. "So, you can't afford to come out a little bit complacent because you think one game's going to be easier than another. So, yes, they were all tough games and obviously because the Olympics were being held there, South Korea had put a lot of resources into their team, and they were dynamite!"

Not only was the structure of the tournament different then, but so too was the way the game itself was structured, as Loretta Dorman remembered. "There was no rotation of players, if you were on you were on for most of the match. You never got subbed, we were in an era where coaches were very reluctant to sub, very much a soccer mentality, where you don't get subbed until the last five or 10 minutes. So, you knew you were there for the long haul in the game, and very rarely did a coach change the team from game to game in that era as well. Potentially if you were in the starting 11, you were on for the whole tournament. So, it was basically a war of attrition to get through it. Every game was like it's do or die, absolutely."

When it came to substitutions, only two were allowed in 1988; three were not permitted for the first time until 1989.

Back in 1988, the game was played on artificial turf, but there were 35-minute halves as opposed to the modern-day 15-minute quarters.

Other than those rules, there was still the offside rule in hockey back in 1988. It wasn't abolished until 1998. In addition, it was not until 1994 that goalkeepers were required to wear protective headgear!

In addition, one of the most important things to remember in 1988 is that a win was only worth two points on the league table.

Day 1

The opening round of games was played on 21 September. Pool A got proceedings under way when Argentina met Great Britain. Moira MacLeod's solitary strike was not only the opening goal of the Games, but also the winner for Great Britain.

Opening the action in Pool B were the hosts South Korea who played West Germany. This game ended in a 4-1 victory for South Korea. Lim Kye-Sook opened the scoring in just the third minute, but West Germany drew level ten minutes later thanks to a goal from Carola Hoffmann.

Just as the Germans were thinking that they were going to head into halftime on level terms, Lim Kye-Sook struck again in injury time.

South Korea's captain Chung Sang-Hyun stretched their lead on the hour, before Seo Kwang-Mi scored a fourth in time added on at the end of the game.

Opening the afternoon session, the Netherlands, the favourites heading into the tournament, defeated the USA 3-1. A penalty corner from Helen Lejeune and a field goal from Sophie von Weiler saw the Dutch head into halftime with a 2-0 lead.

In the 44th minute, the USA pulled a goal back through Sheryl Johnson, but they could not find an equaliser, and when Lisanne Lejeune fired home in the 68th minute, victory was assured for the Dutch.

The last game on day one was Canada v Australia.

For Tracey Belbin, there were mixed emotions.

"I had a cast, not the old plaster of Paris but the newfangled fibreglass or whatever it was, and they put it on, and it was fine. I had some pain and the night before we played Canada, they said we can cut that one off and we'll put this one on. I remember we were out on the bitumen basically and there's Ross, the doc and Brian, and they're getting me to push the ball backwards and forwards and the cast that they put on was actually digging into where the fracture was, and it flared it up. So, then I was ruled out for the game, whereas if I hadn't tried something new, I might have been okay to play."

"Then they put the old cast back on, so for me that first game was all a blur. I remember just sitting on the bench going, 'What's happening?' I should be, I really want to be playing. This is everything I'd been thinking about and what is going on? You get all the psychology with that, because I would run after the game around and around the track, and Brian had to stop me. I remember him saying, 'you don't need to do this, just calm down'. But all I could think was, 'I'm not going to be fit enough, I'm going to lose all this fitness, what if I can't play?'"

According to Captain Debbie Bowman, "every game was pretty intense, and I think that is why we did so well. I think Brian Miller's 'take just one game at a time, let's just get through this one game, let's go through the processes and do the processes one game at a time' really helped, so we never really thought about the gold medal."

"It really didn't feel like we were at the Olympic Games. It was almost like cleaning your teeth in the morning, it was routine. It was like getting up in the morning, brushing your hair and packing your kit. You knew how to warm up, who you were warming up with. There was no up or down of emotion, it was just a case of 'alright, here we go, today we are playing Canada'."

The opening game in any tournament is important. It is vital you do not lose. Everyone wants a win to start their campaign off to ease their nerves.

To make matters worse for Australia being the last to play on that opening day, they were aware of the other results.

The game did not start well. Canada's captain Sheila Forshaw gave her team the lead in just the 12th minute.

"Canada scored early, and they just defended and defended," was Lee Capes' recollection of that game. "They were disruptive and would not allow us to play our game, although this game produced what for me was one highlight of my career. I did a breakaway from the halfway line, ran all the way into the circle, had a shot and was fouled by the goalkeeper and we were awarded a stroke. I can still visualise that one moment, and the ball kept going and going and going and I ended up running half the field, and then I got taken out which was awesome as we got the stroke and scored."

Captain Debbie Bowman stepped forward with 20 minutes remaining and flicked home to pull Australia level.

To many, this would have been a high-pressure moment, but Debbie claimed that after all the preparation the team had done, that was never really the case.

"We did so much practice, and there was a time when we went to the Institute of Sport in Canberra and we were concentrating on strokes. I think that they were trying to work out who could take a stroke under pressure, and they had all these sounds and [a] fake crowd going on around us. In Australia in those days, when a stroke was awarded everything went quiet, and I remember thinking, 'Why have we got all this surround sound?', as no one ever makes any noise at a penalty stroke. 'Why are you making us do this?'"

"Here I was, 'I know everything'! Anyway, I said, 'alright, I will go and do it'. I developed a technique where on a Kookaburra ball there is a picture of a kookaburra, and I placed that kookaburra where I wanted the ball to go as a visual stimulant as to where it was going to go."

"I had learnt the processes of the stroke, so it was more about the direction and not changing my mind, and that kookaburra got me through any stressful situation, even at the Olympic Games, or even State titles. I just knew the processes. I put that kookaburra down where I wanted it to go, and it did not matter what distraction happened after that."

"Obviously, we had also studied the goalkeepers, as to where their strengths and weaknesses were. I would step back and focus on that kookaburra and that kookaburra had to go in that direction, I couldn't change my mind."

Later, Debbie would look back and tell the media that this "was a really awful, nothing game, with no redeeming features".

The game would finish 1-1. Australia had avoided defeat, but more importantly had a point from their opening game.

"Canada then was competitive, and won a medal at a World Cup, and they were coached by two women who had coached the team for a very long time, so they were a tough side to play. But that result was disappointing," was Sharon Buchanan's assessment.

DAY 2

Following a rest day when the men were in action, Australia were first up at 9am for their match against West Germany.

Having lost their opening game, this was do-or-die for West Germany. They needed at least a draw and a win in their remaining games to have any hope of progressing to the semi-finals.

So as expected, this was an extremely tight encounter with neither side giving an inch. Australia dominated the first half with five shots to Germany's one, but the second half was far more even. Both teams went in search of a winner, and West Germany created seven opportunities to Australia's eight.

As they have said for many decades, it only needs one of those chances to go in. That is all that matters. For Australia, that happened in the 68th minute. With just two minutes left on the clock, Debbie Bowman fired home a field goal.

"Against Germany we played some good hockey, there were a lot of factors to take into account – first Olympics for some, quite big crowds, the temperature – but I think we were consistent. We had been consistent as a group and also together as a group for probably 18 months before that," was how Sharon Buchanan looked back on that hard-fought victory.

According to Liane Tooth, this was the team's just reward for sticking to the process and not panicking. "I think often a lot of the goals are scored later in the game because that's when people start to get tired and when you get tired, mistakes creep into the game. So, you've just got to hold it and I think we can give a lot of credit too to our sports psychologist, Brian Miller. That was a new thing for us too, doing sports psychology, but he certainly introduced us to the concept of focusing on the process and not the outcome, and if you do the things you need to do, the outcome will take care of itself, hopefully. But if you start thinking, 'we have to win this or whatever', then you forget about the important things that you need to do to give yourself the chance to win."

Yet it could have been so different. With the game locked at 0-0 and time ebbing away, both teams were looking for that all-important goal to keep their tournament alive.

West Germany was presented with a great opportunity to take the lead as Lee Capes remembered. "I was the first runner at short corners. The defensive battery would line up like this: I was first, my sister Michelle was second, Lianne Tooth, Loretta Dorman and Kath Partridge. Kath always said to me, 'if you think you are close enough, go for it'. So, she always instilled that confidence in me to have a crack. Which is what we did. Everything we did at the Olympics, we had a crack!"

"West Germany won a short corner, and at this short corner I ran out and I wasn't close enough, but I had a crack. I deflected it and Lianne or Loretta was on the post, and it was going straight between their eyes, and they saved it with their stick, which in those days was 'sticks', so gave away a penalty stroke."

"We knew what all their strokers did. But in those days to remember who did what, KP [Kath Partridge] had taped on her cane goalkeeping pads notes she had written telling her where they all went. So, when their number five Dagmar Bremer stepped forward, she looked and it said, 'bottom right'. Bang, she saved it, and we won 1-0 and put Germany out."

This game holds a special memory for assistant coach Peter Freitag. "When we beat Germany, that was one of the times I felt I made a contribution. The Germans were playing in a practice game before the tournament started and I said to Brian, 'I might go out and have a look'. I went out with a couple of the girls, and we sat right at the back of the stand watching the game. We were just about to go at the end of the game when the Germans started practising penalty strokes. So, I wrote down in a diary where each player placed their shot. When we got back to the Village, I went and told Kathy Partridge and she took a note of what I had seen. When we played Germany, she wrote the information on the inside of her pad flap. So, when number five came up to take the stroke, she looked at her notes and knew where it was going to go, and she saved the stroke and we won 1-0. Had we not won that game, we would have only finished on three points, so we would not have played in the final. It was that close."

There are many players who refer to having a slice of luck go their way in major tournaments that is the difference between success and failure. According to Elspeth Denning, this was Australia's moment where luck was on their side.

"We were lucky. You do need a bit of luck and when Germany won a penalty stroke, we had ours. Kath used to write down where her opponents were going when they took a stroke on the inside of her pad and Dagmar – who was a really good friend of mine – stepped forward. We all knew which way she was going. Kath saved it and you could say she won that game for us, or she got us to the final, because that win got us into the final. If that had gone in, it would have changed the game, and if we hadn't scored, we would have been gone, so it all comes down to a bit of luck."

"The tensest game I've played, the Germans needed to win, and although Brian [Glencross] thought we could have survived with a draw, we really had to scrap every inch of the way," was captain Debbie Bowman's comment to the press.

For Rechelle Hawkes, this game was a very different experience. "I think I felt pressure in that one of the games that I played was against Germany. I actually started and I felt the pressure in that game because I knew if I played exceptionally well then, I could be a starter for the rest of the games. But I just played okay, and so then was really on the bench for the rest of the Olympics, as back then it was very much the case of first eleven, and then there was the substitution rule. Once you got taken off, like in soccer, you couldn't come back on. I did get an opportunity, but I didn't really take the opportunity and make the most of it."

On her return to Australia, Kath Partridge talked about the penalty stroke. "Basically, I knew where the shot was going. I had done all the mental work the night before and I had made the stroke dozens of times in my mind. So, when the time came, there were no nerves. I just did it."

"Usually, you look at their eyes. Try to make contact with the person as they start walking up. As soon as they know they are to take it, they generally look once where they are going to put it. If you can pick where they look, at least you know that's where they will go."

In Australia's pool in their second game, South Korea defeated Canada 3-1 thanks to two goals in a minute from Park Soon-Ja, and a third in injury time at the end of the match from Seo Hyo-Sun. Canada pulled a goal back through a Kathryn Johnson penalty corner but were on the back foot for most of the game, creating only four shooting opportunities to South Korea's 19.

In Pool A, Lisanne Lejeune scored three penalty corners and a penalty stroke, and Sophie van Weiler a field goal as the Netherlands tore Great Britain apart 5-1. Britain's consolation goal came from a Vicky Dixon penalty stroke.

Despite the score line, Great Britain created more shooting opportunities in the first half, but either could not beat Bernadette de Beus in goal for the Netherlands or were off target.

In the other match, Argentina kept their tournament hopes alive with a 2-1 victory over the USA. One minute into the second half, Argentina were 2-0 ahead thanks to two penalty corners scored by Cecilia Colombo and Victoria Garbo. The USA, facing an early exit, tried to fight back and Megan Donnelly gave them hope from a penalty corner, but with only nine minutes left on the clock it was too little too late.

DAY 3

Following a day's rest, all eyes were on the women's competition. In Pool A, the Netherlands were top on four points with two wins and had booked their place in the semi-finals. Great Britain and Argentina were both on two points and vying for that other semi-final berth. Great Britain faced a USA side that had yet to win a game, while Argentina was facing the Netherlands.

In Pool B, South Korea were on four points, Australia on three, Canada on one and West Germany on nil. South Korea was assured of a semi-final place, but as they were playing Australia in their final pool game, a loss would see them finish second instead of top. If Canada defeated West Germany and Australia lost, they would be on the same points, and second place would come down to goal difference.

There was certainly plenty at stake for six of the eight teams. Only the USA and West Germany already knew their fate and were playing for pride.

In the opening game of the day, the USA met Great Britain. The British opened the scoring from a penalty stroke converted by Vicky Dixon and carried a 1-0 lead into halftime. Two minutes into the second half, Christy Morgan converted a penalty corner to pull the USA level.

Great Britain reclaimed the lead in the 51st minute when Kate Parker scored a field goal. However, in the last minute, the USA equalised for a second time when Sheryl Johnson converted a penalty corner. They had secured their first point while Great Britain was assured of second spot in Pool A and a place in the semi-finals.

Next up was Canada taking on West Germany, and it was the Germans who took the lead in the 26th minute when Bettina Blumenberg fired home. Canada equalised after halftime when Lisa Lyn converted a penalty stroke.

However, West Germany was not to be denied a first victory and claimed the spoils with nine minutes to go, thanks to a penalty corner from Caren Jungjohann. This victory sealed Australia's place in the semi-finals as Germany leapfrogged Canada into third place.

The Netherlands continued their unbeaten run with a 1-0 win over Argentina, thanks to a Helen Lejeune penalty corner.

Heading into the game against South Korea, the Australians knew they were assured of a semi-final place. But could they claim top spot in Pool B and avoid the Netherlands?

"Our last game was Korea in front of how many thousands and more, because you count the people up the light poles, and there were more there than the official number," Lee Capes remembered. "We knew that the winner of the game avoided playing Holland in the semi-final, and the loser would meet Holland in the semi-final, and if it was a draw, we would have to play Holland. So, there was plenty to play for."

Tracey Belbin admitted that she was purely focused on the game at hand. "I wasn't looking further than the next game, and I think that's the beauty of that tournament and I imagine other people were approaching it similarly. Control what you can control, forget about what you can't, and process the outcome. So, the minute I finished playing West Germany, stepped off the field, then my next thought was South Korea. Okay, 'let's go South Korea'. I remember they'd come to Perth for a practice game four years before that. They played against the AIS team, and I think we beat them something like 12-0, or something ridiculous. So, they just had this incredible improvement, they'd travel all around the world playing games and they had a really strict coach and all the rest of it. So, for them to be so competitive was fantastic."

This was never going to be an easy game, as Elspeth recalled. "The tough game was when we played South Korea, and we had a massive crowd of about

40,000 people who didn't know much about hockey, but who had been told to scream. You could not hear a thing on the pitch. You could call, but your teammate couldn't hear you, it was so loud. It was probably one of the best matches I have ever played in my life, as it was just goal after goal after goal. I remember one of the English commentators saying that it was one of the best games of hockey he had ever seen, up till then obviously."

According to Tracey, it was not just a game that the players would remember for a long time, but also anyone who watched it. "That game was crazy and it's amazing when we got home, the amount of people that said to me, 'oh my God, that was the best game of hockey I've ever seen'. 'I watched the game, I was in an airport', 'I was at my brother's house', 'I was somewhere', 'I stopped in Harvey Norman, I watched that game'. It was an amazing game, and heaps of people said it to me. When we were playing it, it was crazy, it was crazy fast, 10 goals in one game, it was just ridiculous!"

This game was truly one of the most remarkable Olympic matches ever. It was the equivalent of two boxers standing toe-to-toe and neither giving an inch for the entirety of the bout.

There were 37 shots at goal in 70 minutes. An average of a shot at goal just under every two minutes.

Australia appeared to get off to the perfect start when Jackie Pereira opened the scoring with a field goal in just the sixth minute. However, in the 23rd minute, Kim Young-Sook pulled South Korea level with a field goal of her own.

Australia's response was immediate with Debbie Bowman scoring a field goal within a minute of their opponents. The lead was back with Australia.

Then with halftime approaching, two goals in four minutes from Lim Kye-Sook, one from a field goal and then a penalty corner, saw South Korea take the lead for the first time in the match. The crescendo of noise from the crowd was deafening.

Once again, Australia responded immediately. Within a minute, thanks to a Jackie Pereira field goal, they drew level at 3-3. Pereira then gave them the lead as she completed a first half hat-trick with one minute left in the half.

Australia would head into the break with a 4-3 lead. Jackie Pereira, although she did not know it at the time, had become the first Australian woman to score a hat-trick at an Olympic Games.

Remembering that time, she said, "it was very special, because I was the one over the years that they kind of relied on to score goals, and I wasn't scoring every game which was very unlike what I was used to doing. So, for me to get three goals in one game, at least I contributed, but it would have been better if I had shared them around and had a goal in each game to help us a bit, rather than scoring them all in one game!"

"Elspeth always played right back, and I played right half," Tracey recalled, "and we never used to argue. [But] We came off at halftime and we were going at it. Then we're like, 'we just need to calm down, stop being idiots', and you forget whose fault it was and focus on who should be doing what."

Nine minutes into the second half, once again Korea pulled level through their captain Chung Sang-Hyun. A minute later, they took the lead when awarded a penalty stroke. Lim Kye-Sook flicked the ball home to complete her hat-trick and give South Korea the lead 5-4.

If they wanted to avoid the Dutch in the semi-finals, Australia now needed two goals. Suddenly time and not their opponents or the loud raucous crowd became their enemy.

With six minutes left on the clock, they were awarded a penalty stroke.

"We had a penalty stroke earlier in the game and it got saved," Lee Capes recalled, "and so when we had another penalty stroke, we were like, 'Who is going to take this?' Elspeth put her hand up and marched up the field. I don't think she was even in the hierarchy to make that decision, but she was, 'I'll do this', and made it 5-all."

Elspeth remembers the situation a little differently. "We won a penalty stroke and I remember Brian saying to me, 'you take it' and the other coach Peter Freitag saying, 'no, no, not her', and I remember thinking 'Up yours!' I was walking down the pitch going 'Up yours Peter! I am going to take this.' I went up, put it in the back of the net and ran back and gave him a gesture. I was so shitty he said 'no', I was like, 'I'll show you!'" she admitted with a laugh. "That was a great game, it was probably one of the most highly intense games I have ever played."

Peter Freitag did not remember the incident and chuckled when asked about it. However, as a coach, he remembered the game for very different reasons. "That game was like ping-pong. Games are usually built around good defence, and the previous games we had given away no goals in the three practice games, one goal against Canada, and none against Germany. Then we let five in! It was a good learning experience for us. The Koreans were very, very athletic, all go, go, go all the time. They were not sophisticated tactically, but boy they just ran."

It would finish 5-5, and the draw meant that Australia was through to the semi-finals but would meet the team everyone was trying to avoid, the Netherlands.

Looking back on that crucial game, Liane Tooth gave credit to the preparation leading into the tournament and believed that the support staff had done everything right to enable the team to get the outcome they needed on the pitch.

"I think we were pretty fit," she explained. "The Koreans were definitely very fit and used to the whole environment. They were training full-time and used to the turf and the climate, which was pretty hot and humid. But I think we had done a lot of work with our fitness, and I think we held onto that pretty well. I guess the Europeans tend to not play as fast a game either, they tend to be, especially the Germans, more slow and deliberate, building up attacks. We do like to play a faster game; we do like to be aggressive and attack. So, I think that our off-field team had done the right stuff in our preparation, and we were fit and ready to go, and it showed in that game."

Brian Miller, who came in to try and assist in the off-field preparations, shared his view. "We didn't start off that well, we didn't even play that well in the second game, but we won which was good. Then we had a 5-all draw with Korea which was bedlam, just absolutely bonkers. It was the most undisciplined game you have ever seen. So, you could have argued that there had been three pretty ordinary matches, but we did enough to get through. You might argue, and I haven't done the statistics, but if we hadn't done the psychological stuff, maybe the Germany match is a draw, or we lose to Korea and we are out. Who knows? Can I believe it made that much difference? Yes, I can, because we were on the margins, we really were. "Did it get us across the line? I would say yeah, it did. But I say again because they were starting at zero, and had never done any of that stuff before, it had to be better than what they had, and it had to have a small impact."

"They were kind of up for it. Not all the sixteen were. I could rank in order the girls in terms of who believed and who didn't, but it doesn't matter. There were enough who needed this, wanted it and were like, 'thank goodness you are here'. Then he shared with a laugh, "Some of them, some of the older ones, were saying, 'thank goodness you are here, you don't do anything for me, but you keep Brian sane', so that'll do!"

So many athletes will tell you that to win a gold medal, you need a little bit of luck to go your way. Jackie Pereira felt that things fell Australia's way and as easily as they could have been eliminated, the dice fell in their favour this time.

"If you look at the results, we only just managed to get into the finals. Obviously, if we hadn't made the finals, it would have been a very different story. We had to draw or win against South Korea, and we ended up drawing, and then we had to wait on another result, Canada v Germany and the result of that game determined if we were going to go on in the tournament to play in the semis."

"When the results came through, we were all very happy to be in the semi-finals, but knew we were up against the Dutch team, but we weren't as scared as we normally were because we had beaten them recently."

Debbie Bowman was quoted in the press when talking about the South Korean match. *"That really ran the cobwebs out and put us in the right frame of mind. They didn't give us time to think, they just kept on running. It was amazing to have 10 goals in a game, let alone those six in about 10 minutes before halftime. When we came off at the break, I looked over at Tracey, and we didn't want to go back out, being in the middle of it was terrible."*

Semi-Finals

The team had a two-day rest before their semi-final match against the Netherlands. Their game would be the first semi-final to be played starting in the heat of the day at 1pm. The hosts South Korea and Great Britain would meet at 3.15pm.

Three of these four nations would have their men's teams play in the semi-finals that would take place the following day. West Germany would meet the Netherlands, and Australia who had topped their pool would meet Great Britain.

Despite the Dutch being the favourites for the women's gold medal and being the top ranked side, there was now a confidence among the Australians that they could beat them, as Peter Freitag explained. "The Dutch at that time had the reputation of being the best in the world, but we had beaten them in Perth in March of that year. That was a huge moment to beat them in Perth. I remember we had a big crowd for what was a big game out at the Hockey Stadium, and I think when we beat them, it put in the girl's minds, 'yes we are good, yes we can win medals'. It was a huge turning point."

It clearly was as Michelle Capes remembers feeling going into this game. "I remember always going, 'oh God, we're playing the Dutch, and we're going to play but we probably won't win'. I think that was our attitude because we knew that they were so good, and we hadn't beaten them for so long. Then we played a game in Perth, and we beat them and then it was like, 'oh, actually they are beatable'. I've never played with another team like this one, but you just knew that if we did what we needed to do properly, and go through our processes, and trust one another, which we did, we could actually beat them. You know, not so much worry about them, but focus more on what we need to do, and we did. We had a very good psychologist back then and he wasn't all about psyching yourself up and all that stuff. It was more about the processes and dealing with, 'What if that happens?' It was more as a team, let's get together and let's do it together and if we do it together and we do it the way we should do it, it will work."

Rechelle Hawkes agreed with this view. "I did sense that because the Netherlands were very much the benchmark and we'd had the '86 World Cup in the Netherlands where they won, and we'd finished a disappointing sixth. We'd had a couple of games against them in which they'd always dominated us, and I think that quite rightly, and it was pointed out to us that that win [in Perth in 1988] was a bit of a turning point because it did create that belief. Because you tend to always be chasing the number one-ranked team, and they do intimidate the opposition. So, very much that was a turning point [in Perth] and did create that belief within the team."

According to Kim Small, it wasn't just the victory in Perth that gave the team confidence, but that they had done so with a key player missing. "Our team had been together for about three years, so the combinations were there, the belief was there after the Esanda tournament, and if I remember correctly, we didn't have Jackie at that tournament, she was injured. So that was a big benefit going into the Olympics having just beaten them and with Jackie back in the team. Once you have that belief, it certainly helps coming into the next game against that same opposition."

Captain Debbie Bowman has no doubts that the victory in Perth saw the team head into the Olympic semi-final with a very different attitude. "I totally agree, the belief was so much higher. They were so easily the best team in the world, and because they could play the countries beside them on a weekend, they could go to Germany or Belgium, they were idolized. They were like Brazil in soccer. So, when we beat them in Perth, we kind of shocked ourselves, but we also had a belief then that we have done it once, we can do it again. But we had to stay with what we knew was the right thing to do. We couldn't allow them to get into our game. We did a lot of jinking over the European's sticks; this was all planned. These were not traditional Australian skills, they were very low, and we were very upright players. We spent hours and hours changing our thought processes, and practising so that we could drag the ball around them and give good ball to each other."

Elspeth said, "I remember speaking to the girls before that game and saying we can get a medal here. We've got nothing to lose. They are the team to beat, [if] we lose, well we are expected to lose, but if we win, we are in the final. I think everyone went into that game with that attitude. 'No one thinks we are going to win, but we are going to go out there and give it everything we've got, and if we lose, we were meant to lose.' That was the attitude and that is what we did."

According to Lee Capes, there was a real unity among the team, but not only were they united, there was a belief that they were going to win this game. "I remember going out onto the pitch and the whole team feeling, 'we've got nothing to lose. We've done this before and we can do it again.' There was just such a belief. There wasn't nerves, there were no nerves at all, we had such a belief."

"I remember that game quite fondly because I scored a goal from a penalty corner which I hadn't done a lot," Liane Tooth admitted. It was her goal in the third minute that gave Australia the lead against the defending Olympic champions.

"That obviously gives you a really good boost to start a game off like that," she added. "It just gives you a bit of extra. You're already starting to have that belief that the Dutch are no longer the dominant team, and that you can match it with them. To have a start like that in a semi-final is kind of a dream start for you. It just gives you a bit of extra confidence on top of that belief that you already had."

"Going 1-0 ahead after three minutes was a real bonus. We decided to go with a different corner combination, but practising just before the game, we couldn't get it right, bad hit-ins, I was missing the traps, and Liane was mishitting. It just all came together in the first corner we had, and Liane hit it like a bullet," Debbie remembered.

However, the team's belief was tested in the 16th minute when the Dutch had a penalty corner of their own and Lisanne Lejeune pulled the Dutch level at 1-1.

Despite the Dutch having 21 shots to Australia's nine, that was how the score remained up until halftime.

Thirteen minutes after the break, Sharon Buchanan restored Australia's lead, and then eight minutes later, she doubled it. When pressed on recollections of her two goals, Sharon modestly responded. "Yeah I remember them. I was a midfielder, but every tournament I set myself a goal to score a minimum of two goals. So obviously you do a lot more work, a lot more running, and I had more time on the pitch, but it isn't always easy to score, so to score them against Holland was special. In big games, you have to stand up."

While many dream of scoring a brace in an Olympic semi-final, for Tracey, all her dreams came through making the pass to Sharon. "When we played them in the semi-final, one of my best memories is when I set up the goal for Sharon and she scored. For me, that is one of the best moments of my playing career because I remember the feeling, having passed the ball to her and seeing her score. I just wanted to cry on the field. I was just filled with so much emotion, and so proud and so passionate. I knew then that we were going to win this game and were going to be in a final for our country. That was one of my best moments ever. I was really emotional on the field, and kind of had to pull myself together to finish off the game."

It came as no surprise that the Dutch threw everything at the Australians. Kath Partridge and every single player on the field defended valiantly. With nine minutes to go, the Dutch won a penalty corner. Their captain Marjolein Bolhuis-Eljsvogel scored, and the Dutch had a lifeline – the chance to score an equaliser and take the game into extra time.

"Jitters? Oh yes, there were jitters!" Sharon Buchanan admitted. "Right to the end. It was a tough match, but it was 3-1 for most of the match. I can't remember the end of the match, whether we were hanging on or not. I honestly can't remember, but I think we stuck to our game plan which was really good, and it paid off."

The final whistle sounded and Australia had won. They were into the Olympic final. The reigning Olympic gold medallists would be playing for bronze. This was a huge moment not just for hockey, but also for women's team sport.

"It was so close. We got the third goal which was an important cushion," Elspeth remembered. "They were devastated, they couldn't believe they had lost. They were the cream of the cream, the Dutch in that era. They were so good, no one could beat them. There weren't even lucky wins over them, you just couldn't beat them. I remember when you played them, you would walk out and think, 'ugh we're going to get flogged'. Looking back, I think we went into that game thinking we had nothing to lose, and because we were so close, we all worked so hard for each other."

"When we beat the Dutch in the semi-final, I remember going up and hugging Sharon. In those days, male coaches could hug female players," Peter

Freitag remembered. "We were both thinking, 'we are going to go home with a medal! Whatever happened now we have got something to go home with.' I think this kind of made up for LA, where they had played really well and came home with nothing and went home sad and angry. When we beat the Dutch 3-2, the rejoicing was overwhelming, the realisation that they had done something here, and that was not just to win a medal. We knew what the Koreans were like, and we had time to think through how we were going to approach that game. I remember the relief. It was almost a more significant moment than winning the gold, almost! To go home with nothing would have been tragic. To win this match meant we were going to be in the gold medal game with the world watching. It was all a big deal."

The West Australian newspaper's Len Findlay reported: *"Patmore with tears in her eyes told coach Brian Glencross after the match "I saved them up for you." These were Sharon's first two goals of the tournament, and they could not have come at a more important time. Although she could well have scored a hat-trick with two minutes to go, but at the end of the day the result was all that mattered."*

"We were pretty excited," was Liane Tooth's memory of the immediate aftermath and the realisation that the team would be playing off for an Olympic gold medal. "I guess it was about enjoying that moment, but then being able to get your mind back into focus. Obviously by the time you get to the actual gold medal game, you've got to put that last game to bed, so that you're able to focus on what you need to do. So, looking ahead to the game against Korea, obviously there were some learnings to take away from the round game that went to 5-5. But yeah, it was a pretty exciting time, to know that we were going to be in a gold medal game. None of us wanted silver, but it was good to know it was the worst that you could do."

All the focus had been on reaching this point. "I think the pressure was off, but even though that was the case, we knew we were in for a tough match because of the round game we had played against Korea," Kim Small reflected. "We knew it was going to be as fast as you would ever want. I think it may have been a different story had we played the Netherlands in the gold-medal match. We knew we could beat South Korea, so I think we were staying positive the whole way up to the final match day."

"I remember, we'd joke in our rooms, 'oh, the guys are in the media, they're on TV et cetera', and in hindsight that was probably good. That was probably one of the positives for us, as it meant that we kind of flew under the radar a bit," Tracey revealed. "No one thought that we could win or would win. The guys took all the heat. So, when we beat the Dutch... I guess that was the turning point."

For Elspeth, the semi-final was her 100th match for Australia. She became the first woman to reach that milestone. There was almost symmetry to it being her 100th game, as it was in her 50th game that she broke her hand, an injury that resulted in her missing playing at the Los Angeles Olympics.

Brian Glencross revealed after the semi-final win that "it is my proudest moment in sport. It has to be. We are playing off for the gold medal in the Olympic Games."

The team had three days' rest until the gold-medal match. Three days to let the victory sink in and start focusing on the final.

It was sad that the Australian press picked up on the comments of the Dutch coach Gys van Heuman, who was quoted as saying: *"This is the end of an era. This is the first time in eight years The Netherlands has not been in a final. We played very badly... I don't think you could say the Australians played very well to beat us."*

Rather than praise the Australian team for stopping an incredible run by the Netherlands, and possibly crediting the Australian team with not allowing the Dutch to play as they wanted to, many media outlets chose to downplay the victory on the back of the losing coach's words. They followed his line that this Dutch team was not as good as those in the past, and that was the only reason the Australians had won.

In defence of their team, the Australian coaching staff were quick to point out that the Netherlands can't have been that bad if they beat another semi-finalist (Great Britain) 5-1 in the pool stage.

Glencross was also quick to point out that the Olympic semi-final win was Australia's second win in their last two games against the Dutch. It was down to persistence and perseverance. He saw the first win in the final of the Esanda Cup in Perth as crucial.

"That win in Perth proved we had rid ourselves of the great phobia the Netherlands had over everyone. Our secret today was to keep to our game plan, not to fall into theirs. I was emphatic that we keep the ball moving with short passes and that we kept it moving," Glencross said post-game. When asked if he was worried as the Dutch piled on the pressure in the last 20 minutes, his response was a classic. "I was more concerned by the umpires!"

The team had to wait to find out who their opponent would be in the final, as South Korea played Great Britain after their semi-final finished. A single field goal in the 18th minute from Seo Hyo-Sun was enough to secure South Korea's place in the gold-medal match.

The following day, 28 September, proved to be another bad day for the Netherlands as their men bowed out in the semi-finals as well, going down 2-1 to West Germany.

Australia had a chance of both teams playing for gold, but it wasn't to be as the men lost 3-2 to Great Britain. Sean Kerly completed his hat-trick and booked his team a place in the gold- medal match in the 67th minute.

For Brian Miller, the team psychologist, everything was going according to plan. "By the time we came to play against the Dutch, who let's be honest were a superhuman force, we'd done just enough in the group stages. The cunning plan was just to get through that; whereas the boys' team did fantastically in the group stage and then had nowhere to go. We had done enough and were still keeping some of the powder dry. I was surprisingly confident against the Dutch but then I was not so confident going up against the Koreans, because they were at home, and the crowd and all that stuff, but the girls seemed incredibly confident."

Yet despite the women making the gold-medal match and the men being forced to play off for bronze, the newspapers in Australia again tended to focus on the men's game, and some could be a little condescending towards the women.

One report opened with the following: *"Australia may finally win its first Olympic hockey gold medal today, but it will not be the men's team, five times world champions and tournament favourites, who do it. After losing their semi-final against Great Britain 3-2, the Australian men have again failed in the only top tournament they have not mastered. Now it is up to the women. After winning their semi against the Netherlands 3-2, the women are assured of a gold or silver medal in the final against Korea."*

However, the same report did in fact echo the opinion of Brian Miller when it stated: *"Seeded second in this Olympics, the women had a slow start to the tournament, drawing 1-1 with Canada and narrowly beating West Germany 1-0 before the game with Korea. But they improved markedly with every game and deserved their semi-final win over the Dutch. That win was extra sweet because not only was it the first time the Australian women had made it to an Olympic final, but they had done it by toppling the team which has dominated women's hockey for the past eight years."*

5. THE GOLD-MEDAL MATCH

*"The moment of victory is much too short to live for that,
and nothing else."*

Czech-born US tennis player Martina Navratilova

"We were relaxed going into this game, because we had a silver medal," Elspeth said, and her view was shared by most of the team. "Sandy and Loretta were the two jokers in the team, and they kept everything light-hearted leading into the final, and that made a big difference."

"I think the mood did change a bit because it was the final, but I still remember saying, 'we've got a silver medal, we're OK', we had that guaranteed. However, it is different when you go into a final, it's a very different game. We knew that they were really good, we knew how fast they were and Brian came up with ways for us to counteract how they played. On the day, we just played our own game."

"They hadn't beaten us," Sharon remembered thinking. "A draw was the closest they had managed for a few years. We always seemed to have the wood over them, so we were confident in that way, but Olympic final is very different. I can't remember ever being as nervous as I was going into that match. You had to use every strategy that we had been taught to keep our emotions together and stay focused on what the goal was."

Brian Glencross said in the press prior to the Olympic final that he expected this game to be very different from their earlier encounter.

"I think it will be a very different encounter from the first one. Neither side is going to give that much away in the goals department. They know what to expect from each other and the defence and the tactics will be different. Well, ours will be at least. Obviously, I don't know what the Koreans will do, but I can tell you one thing, it's going to be very tough and very close."

The team knew from their previous encounter that the crowd were going to be extremely partisan towards South Korea, but the squad and support staff had prepared them for that in Canberra.

"I think we'd already kind of got used to the crowd and some of the rent-a-crowd that made noises when there wasn't really anything happening," Liane said. "We had done that in our lead-up when we had our training camp in Canberra, of all places. That prepared us as they put all these speakers around the pitch, and they had this recording of crowd noise and played that really loudly through all our games to get us used to the fact that it might be very hard to hear your teammates on the field when we got to Korea. I think, in terms of once we were at the Olympics, we simply shut the crowd out."

It has come to light that apart from this preparation in camp in Canberra, the Australians would try anything to lessen the impact of the crowd. Apparently, team psychologist Brian Miller and friends did what they could to sway some of the Korean crowd to support Australia! Toy koalas, and kangaroo pins were handed out to members of the crowd in the hope that they may cheer for Australia and "quite a few United States dollars changed hands" with the crew of the public-address system to have Australia's Olympic song, *You're Not Alone*, played before the match.

The first real opportunity of the match came Australia's way. Elspeth Denning stole possession just inside Korea's half. Quick passing saw Liane Tooth play the ball forward to Lee Capes who passed to Jackie Pereira who played the ball straight back to the advancing Capes. She surged into the circle and along the baseline, and tried to play the ball back to Pereira, but good anticipation by goalkeeper Chung Eun Kyung saw Korea snuff out the attack.

Korea then went on a strong attack of their own with Park Soon Ja heavily involved as they passed their way through the midfield. The final pass into the circle by their captain Chung Sang Hyun had too much pace on it and ran harmlessly into the goal. However, being unaware of the rules, the crowd roared in celebration.

With eight minutes gone, Australia won a penalty corner. The Koreans broke early, so it was retaken. Kim Small played the ball in, Loretta Dorman stick-stopped it, and Liane Tooth shot at goal, but again the Korean goalkeeper saved well and deflected the ball wide for a long corner.

Five minutes later, it was Korea who found a way in behind the Australian defence. Kim Young Sook played the ball to the advancing Lim Kye Sook who passed back to the penalty spot where Australia scrambled it clear.

The opening 15 minutes had seen both teams looking to attack at every opportunity, but so far neither had been able to break the deadlock. Australia's defence was marking much tighter than in the earlier encounter and giving the Koreans little time or space when they did enter the circle.

From the 20-minute mark Korea poured forward, and it was only some well-timed tackles by Tracey Belbin, Michelle Capes and Elspeth Denning that kept them at bay.

Then from a tackle inside her own circle, Elspeth found Debbie Bowman and Australia were able to launch a counterattack. Her pass found the pacey Lee Capes who played the ball infield from the left-hand side. It went behind Pereira, no doubt deliberately, as it ran perfectly into the path of the advancing Kim Small. Small beat three defenders and played the ball towards goal, but once again the Korean goalkeeper, Chung Eun Kyung, cleared.

Both teams continued to look to attack, but their passing either faltered around the circle or the defence intercepted.

With 25 minutes gone in the first half a great opportunity to break the deadlock before halftime fell to Jackie Pereira. A turnover by Korea saw an early pass played by Kim Small to Pereira who had ghosted in behind the defence at the top of the circle. She took one touch, but the Korean goalkeeper had come a long way and closed her down as she tried to shoot. The ball ricocheted back to Australia, Small tried to play it over to the right-hand side, but Korea intercepted. The clearance went straight back to Small who ran towards goal but the best she could do was win another penalty corner.

Once again, the Koreans broke early; there was no reduction of defenders for such an offence in 1988. At the second attempt, Tooth shot but the logging Chung Eun Kyung saved. The rebound came to Pereira but the keeper made another superb save while still prostrate on the ground. The ball came back to Pereira again, she tried to lift it over the keeper, but the ball was prevented from entering the goal by the leg of a defender and umpire Salobar Hernandez pointed to the penalty spot.

Tracey Belbin stepped forward to take the stroke, the third Australian to do so in the tournament. The Korean goalkeeper took her time to be ready. The crowd noise grew to a crescendo. They were so loud that it was hard to hear the whistle. It sounded. Belbin took the one step and flicked to the goalkeeper's right but Chung pulled off a superb save. A save that meant the crowd roared even louder. As Chung lay on the turf reflecting how crucial it may be, her teammates came running back to congratulate her. A game can turn on such moments.

On the half-hour mark, Park Soon Ja received the ball on the left and carried it into the circle where she managed to get the better of Elspeth Denning. She continued her run towards goal and Kath Partridge, then slipped the ball back, but Korea shot wide.

Park was the creator again for Korea minutes later when receiving the ball in space on the left. She took one touch and set up an early forehand pass to Lim Hye Sook on the right flank. As she looked to carry the ball into the circle, Michelle Capes swooped and stole it away cleanly before feeding it to Bowman. Bowman then played a good one-two with Pereira, before Pereira passed to Small at the top of the circle and continued her run looking for the return pass. The perfect pass came from Small, but unfortunately Pereira had gone a little too early and was deemed offside.

With two minutes to go until the break, Small smashed a ball into the circle from the right with both Lee Capes and Pereira poised in front of goal to deflect it home, but it whistled past both of their sticks. Korea would mount one more attack before the hooter, but once again resolute defending kept them at bay and the teams headed in for the halftime break at 0-0.

Australia was on the front foot as soon as the second half commenced. Sharon Buchanan went on a mazy run towards the circle, beating two players before being dispossessed by a third. Then it was Kim Small who created some space after good work down the right and she had the Korean defence scrambling.

Two minutes into the half, the Australians won their third penalty corner. The ball in was not a good one, but Loretta Dorman trapped it and then caught almost everyone by surprise by pushing a shot at goal. Luckily for Korea, Chung Eun Kyung was aware of the danger and threw herself to her left to deflect the shot wide.

Another penalty corner came Australia's way just after five minutes of the second half had elapsed. This was Australia's fourth. The ball was played out to Elspeth Denning, who fired a powerful shot that beat the goalkeeper but was prevented from entering the goal by Korean captain Chung Sang Hyun's foot. The whistle blew and Australia was awarded a second penalty stroke. The question was, who would take this one?

Captain Debbie Bowman stepped forward, having scored one and missed one in the tournament. Never was it more important that she score. Bowman flicked to the goalkeeper's right. Chung threw herself in the same direction, but this time the ball flew past her, hit the back of the net and came rebounding out of the goal.

Bowman turned and immediately ran back to her teammates, urging them to carry on with the intensity they had come out with in the second half. Australia was leading 1-0 with 29 minutes remaining!

"I was elated to score after missing one in our previous drawn game with Korea. I just turned off to all the boos from the crowd and flicked it in," she said.

Not surprisingly, Korea lifted, and a surging penetrative run by Kim Young Sook was only thwarted by a last-ditch tackle by Liane Tooth.

With 26 minutes left on the clock, Debbie Bowman found Lee Capes on the left-hand side in space. Capes sped forward, ran around the ball and struck it into the circle. Jackie Pereira knew exactly where it was going and had made a superbly timed run to the near post. She deflected the ball towards goal, but once again Chung had read the play well and came off her line to close down the angle and make a very good save.

However, Korea only half-cleared, and Michelle Capes immediately played a pass to Kim Small who was unmarked on the right. The ball took a fortuitous deflection and Small had a clear run at goal. Unselfishly, she squared the ball to Jackie Pereira just five metres in front of goal, but once again the Korean goalkeeper denied Australia.

Korea kept pressing and Australia kept them at bay. On one occasion in her desperation to clear, Lee Capes lifted the ball and struck Chang Eun Jung in the face. Play was held up as she received treatment before leaving the field of play.

Korea continued to press and the crowd continued to roar, but the Australian defence held firm and prevented a meaningful shot at goal.

With 20 minutes left, Australia broke forward and Korea only half-cleared. The ball fell to Small just inside the circle on the right and she hit a first-time shot with power towards goal, but once again Chung was there to save.

Within seconds, Korea were on the attack Chung Sang Hyun played a defence-splitting pass into the path of Lim Kye Sook. Australia's defence seemed to hesitate, believing that Lim was offside, but luckily after a moment's hesitation, Kath Partridge was off her line in a flash to block Lim's tame attempt at goal.

Every attack from Korea was urged on by the local crowd, and the noise they made was deafening. With a quarter-of-an hour left, a wonderful passing move by Korea looked threatening, but was broken up by Tracey Belbin.

Two minutes later, Australia played the ball forward. Jackie Pereira deflected the ball to Lee Capes who still had a lot to do, but again ran around the ball and struck it with power past Chung in goal to stretch Australia's lead to 2-0!

However, unfortunately for those watching in Australia, that crucial moment was missed as Channel 10 had gone to a commercial break!

"What was interesting was that there were four girls from my club team Pirates – now Curtin University – in the Australian team," Lee recalled. "That goal was created at our club. I have always stressed the importance of learning to play with your teammates, staying in little groups and following each other through. Staying together as a group and learning from each other, and about each other, and how to play together can see you go to all sorts of amazing heights."

"Leading up to that goal, my sister Michelle made the tackle and won the free hit, Elspeth took the free hit and played the ball to Jackie, who deflected it, and I picked it up and got the goal. That was the four Pirates' girls. It was amazing when you think about it."

Remembering this second goal, Peter Freitag made a confession. "Jackie Pereira deflected it and Lee hit it through the goalie's legs and I thought 2-0 up, we are going to win! I always thought about writing a pretend book and having it next to me, and on the cover, it would say *How to Win a Gold Medal*. But I thought, 'what a prick I would have looked if we lost', but ever since that day, I wish I had done it."

Australia deprived South Korea of possession after the restart but when they did win the ball back, the Koreans continued to test the Australian defence. But with every attack, an Australian would snuff it out with a well-timed tackle.

The game had less than 10 minutes remaining, and while most sports fans would expect the drama to be on the pitch, it was happening on the sidelines for the Australian women.

The team knew that time was ticking away, and that Maree Fish and Lorraine Hillas had to get on the field of play or they would not receive a medal.

The day before the final, an official had presented the Australian team with a copy of rule 64 of the Olympic Charter which indicated that the two players had to be on the field of play for at least 30 seconds to be eligible to receive a medal.

The actual wording read as follows: *"each member of a winning team participating in at least one match shall be awarded a silver gilt [gold] medal and a diploma, each member of the second team a silver medal and a diploma and each member of the third team a bronze medal and a diploma."* It went on to say that *"the other members of these teams are awarded diplomas but no medals".*

Australia should have been well aware of this rule as in the men's final in

Montreal in 1976, Steve Marshall was not given a silver medal as he had not stepped onto the pitch. For gold medallists' New Zealand, two players were also refused medals for the same reason – reserve goalkeeper Les Wilson and Neil McLeod. Marshall did manage to dodge security and stand on the podium with his teammates, but he was not presented with a medal. However, Australian team captain Bob Haigh, who had also won silver in 1968 at the Mexico Olympics, generously gave Marshall his medal.

Many believed the rule had been changed following 1976, as in 1984 Great Britain goalkeeper Vern Pappin received a bronze medal despite not having played a game. When this matter raised its ugly head again in 1988, there was talk that Pappin would be asked to return his medal. Press reports claimed that he had said if he was asked, he would decline, and quite rightly so.

Brian Miller remembered the discussions before the final only too well. "I was involved with the men's team a bit, the women's team, and athletics in Seoul, and athletics was very much the second week. So, I was running from pillar to post and then we had a team meeting in between the Dutch semi-final and the gold-medal match where there was a discussion which took place, and someone said, 'it would be better to have 16 silvers than 14 gold'. I'd rocked up all sweaty after rushing to be there and probably grumpy as well because they were long days in Seoul, and someone mentioned this, and I went ballistic. This was a program that was only focused on gold medals, and I said, 'No it is 16, but we are only talking about gold medals, 16 gold medals!' But again, it showed the unity in that group to even think that way."

"Clearly, whoever made these rules had no understanding of what it means to be a part of a sporting squad at a tournament or the stress it would cause."

"The great rugby coach Sir Ian McGeechan revealed that as a coach you have an idea of who your main starting line-up will be, but he made it very clear that the last selections in a squad are critical."

"*These are the players who are really good at doing the bits and pieces all the time, fitting in, and making the tour work. They are really strong characters in a different way. You feel they can add value, perhaps in unexpected ways, the type who won't go off on tour, won't get too down and won't upset things. They determine the chemistry and environment of the tour, how quickly it builds and how strong it becomes,*" he wrote *in The Lions When the Going Gets Tough*. He finished by saying, *"They can make or break a tour."*

"Every single player has said how important Lorraine and Maree were as part of the squad, and the unity shown towards them is a credit to them as individuals. They could have moaned that they were not getting a game. They didn't and put the greater good of the team first. They epitomised what Sir Ian was talking about."

"I kept saying to Brian when we had selection meetings, get them on the field early," Elspeth recalled. "'Oh no, what happens if we get an injury', was Brian's reply. Remember, there was no interchange then."

"'Get them on early so you can replace them', I would tell him, but he kept saying, 'What happens if I get an injury?' and I was, 'Oh God!' I could never win that argument. Every game was crucial, as you can see, so I think it was very hard for him."

"Brian absolutely 100 per cent had it squared away with the Dutch TD [Technical Director]. Those girls were going on," Brian Miller revealed. "The nervousness was how late can anyone ever leave it? Certainly, Elspeth was getting really stroppy, shouting and being rude to him. He did have it all under control, he just necessarily hadn't shared all those details with the players because obviously the focus was on the gold medal."

Elspeth did not shy away from the fact that she was yelling at the coach. "With five minutes to go, I remember shouting at the bench, saying, 'Get me off the field, get them on!' I was screaming at the coach and pysch. I admit I lost all interest in the game. I was screaming at them, and they were yelling at me to concentrate on the game, and I was just saying, 'Get them on!'"

"Then Kathy started yelling, as Maree was a goalkeeper, and she knew that if she did not get on, she didn't get a medal. Then I said, 'I am going down injured', and Brian was shouting, 'no, no, I will get her on'. There were less than two minutes left when he got them on the field, I could have shot him."

"I remember Elspeth in particular, and then everyone started going, "Get them on, get them on, get them on!" That was how Loretta Dorman recalled this stage of the gold-medal match. "I remember before the game, it's in the back of your mind that you want everyone to be successful, and this was a way to be successful, wasn't it? To show that they were there, and they were a part of this special group. So, to mark the occasion, it was absolutely vital they got on. Since then, they've changed the rules, which is good, but back then, it was definitely a bit stressful. It's made me get a bit teary talking about it, because it was a very poignant moment in the whole campaign. It showed how united we were as a group."

For Maree, the longer the game went, the better it was for her. "For me to get on as a goalkeeper was a bit challenging. The other thing that was in play and the players didn't really know this, and I am flabbergasted they didn't, I am pretty sure Debbie Bowman would have known, as she was the captain and her and I roomed together, but she wasn't in the group when we were talking about this. I actually had Ken Wark's shirt from the men's team, he was number 16 and I had a skirt in my bag so that I could come on as a field player if necessary, but I desperately did not want to. I needed probably about 8-10 minutes to change out of my goalkeeping kit, so I was overjoyed when five minutes to go came along, because that meant I would not have enough time to change and come on as an outfield player."

Lorraine Hillas remembered that she had "warmed up an awful lot. We would run up and down and not get on the pitch," she laughed at the memory and then revealed how she had complete faith in those out on the pitch. "I don't recall thinking that I thought the girls would stuff it up. I thought we were playing great hockey and I always thought we would win it and we had the team to win it."

She remembered Brian Miller coming up to her on the morning of the final and saying, "you have to go on to win a medal". I said, "I know that."

"I remember the video cameras were trying to get a shot of me because it was getting later and later in the game, and it was looking like I wouldn't get on. Rechelle, Sandy and Sally were trying to stand in the way and block the camera so they could not see me. It was hilarious really."

"Brian was standing on the side and the poor old TD [Els van Breda Vriesman] from the Netherlands kept looking across, as she knew the situation and was desperate to get us on the pitch. Kathy Partridge and Elspeth were yelling across to Brian. Apparently, they were having a discussion that they were both going to go down injured to get us on. It was so cool how close we all were, and how everyone was pulling together to get us on."

Lorraine paused for a moment remembering what must have been an incredibly emotional time.

"Brian [Glencross] was going, 'not yet, not yet' to the umpire. I am not proud of this, but it was the only time I ever swore at a coach in my career, as I strongly asked him what I could do wrong in two minutes? I remember thinking, "oh God I've just sworn at the coach', which was something I never did."

Brian Miller was quick to defend this out-of-character behaviour from Lorraine. "In her defence, and it is easy with hindsight, there were opportunities in the group matches where she could have gone on for a few minutes. It was not like she was a rubbish player, she deserved to be there. She was a perfectly competent player. We forget it was different then, and I am not sure the penny completely dropped until we got to the semi-final and only then we started to talk about it and how everyone had to get on the pitch to get a medal."

These were moments that Sally Carbon says she will never forget. "Rechelle was on the bench next to me, the two of us were sitting there, but we knew that we weren't going to play. For us to go on, it meant that our teammates wouldn't have gone on. So, we went to the game knowing that we weren't going to play. I have never seen anything like it before or since. Honestly, it was like this game of hockey was going on with busy ants running about, but our entire team was screaming at Brian, and everyone on the bench was screaming at Brian, and who knows who held the game together on the pitch."

Brian Miller, who had worked so hard to give the team belief and focus, admitted that there were nerves on the side as "I think the whole team had lost focus by then, luckily, we were up," he remembered.

There were even some nerves on the pitch as Lee Capes recalled. "Tracey Belbin had the ball in the last three minutes, and she was our most skilful player, and she had it in the corner playing with it trying to kill time. Tracey was right half so because she had gone forward with the ball and as I was right wing, it meant that I had to drop in at right half to cover her. That was really scary."

Sharon Buchanan felt equally nervous. "I remember the last five minutes as there was quite a bit of emotion around, and in the last couple of minutes we just held the ball in the corner." She remembered with a laugh, "I hate doing that, but on that occasion, it was a case of too bad!"

Even Tracey felt the pressure, and she had the ball! "I remember in the last couple of minutes, we were saying, 'keep the ball, keep the ball'. Back then, we never really ran across the other side of the field, not like they do in today's game, but I remember Michelle saying, 'come and get the ball' so that I could keep it. You know, just hold it for a couple of minutes. I remember that so clearly and, yeah, it was nerve-wracking, because they were a very good team."

"I remember feeling really anxious as we were 2-0 up, and there were only a couple of minutes to go, and we knew that Maree and Lorraine had to come on. I think for me, and I imagine for everyone else, that was the priority in our thoughts. We needed to get them on. I remember Elspeth yelling out, 'someone go down, someone go down with an injury, someone go down'. Then Maree came on."

Eventually, the substitutions were made with one minute and 35 seconds left on the clock. "I went on for Kim Small," Lorraine remembered. "In those days, only the strikers ever came off, so if you were a half back, you never got subbed. The defence usually stayed on, and so the strikers were the ones who came off. So, the chance of Sally and Rechelle getting a gig was much higher than mine. You just have to be prepared when you get that chance. I did think I would get a goal. I had a dream where I scored," Lorraine laughed before adding "even if I was only on for two minutes! I got the ball a couple of times, and it's history now."

"I am actually quite grateful as they could have picked someone else to be over there. I would have still been close to the same people, Sharon and Rechelle are godmothers to my children, and Elspeth, Sally and I are really close, so I would still have been close friends, but having been there, I am now forever a part of something that is really, really, special."

"I had such a new respect for Maree, and I only found out at one of our reunions that she had a playing uniform in her bag from one of the men in case she had to come on the field," Tracey Belbin revealed. "That's crazy stuff and I was like, 'What? We didn't know about that?' Then when she came on, the Koreans got a corner and these guys can score in seven seconds, they're so quick and skilful. Maree hadn't touched the ball, she hadn't played for two weeks, and then they belted it at her, and she made this fantastic save, and I was like, 'What the hell?' To me, that was amazing, really amazing. The resilience and the strength of mind she had to do that in that environment, and that particular stage of the game, was amazing. That's what I remember about the game, the last minutes for me were like everyone was kind of panicking a bit because we needed to get Maree and Lorraine on so that they get a medal too."

"Maree made a crucial save and she hadn't played one minute of one game," Elspeth said. "Remarkable, truly remarkable."

Brian Miller remembered that save too. "She did make a save, or maybe two saves. She was a decent goalkeeper so that was hardly a surprise, but to go on and make those saves, also given the slight embarrassment that both Lorraine and Maree felt going on for this last hoorah is a credit to her to have been mentally in the zone."

"They thoroughly deserved their medals, and it is illogical for anyone to say that they don't," Brian added. "They had been in the team in all the games leading up to then and had made a contribution on and off the pitch. Of course, today with rolling subs, it's not a topic anymore."

Assistant coach Peter Freitag also remembered Maree's save. "Had they scored with two minutes to go, who knows what would have happened. It was a very important save and once we cleared the ball, it meant that we were going to win. I think that save is underrated. We were all thinking 'the gold medal is ours' when she came on. Had they scored, it could have changed everything."

"We knew before that game they would not get medals if they had not taken the field, which I thought was ridiculous. When Maree made that save, it was like, 'yep we've done it, and everyone has played their part!'"

Maree had a much more matter-of-fact view of those final minutes. "I made a save and after me, Lorraine got a touch, so it all worked out perfectly for the both of us."

Although she did reveal that sharing a room with Debbie had helped her to stay focused during the Games. "You train and every time the team is announced, you hope that you might get on today, but we only played five games. Debbie was focused. She wasn't going to muck around, she was a very focused lady, but saying that, we still had a bit of banter. There is not a lot of down time when you are there because you do not want to go off to the city too much and run yourself ragged because you still have to play, and you are still training. When we had been there the year before, we would go to the shopping mall, but in '88 we were much more focused, and I found I needed to support her to stay focused myself."

"They were so important to the team," Elspeth explained. "These two were the perfect teammates. While many players, especially women would have moaned and bitched about not playing, Lorraine and Maree never did once. The whole time they supported everyone else. I shared an apartment with Rechelle, Sally and Lorraine, and Lorraine kept me relaxed. She made me laugh and had me in stitches at times. Staying relaxed was so important. They were always going to get on as Kath and I were going down injured, and Brian knew that."

Kim Small, who made way for Lorraine, summed up everything simply. "The substitution issue was a debacle. Things are done differently these days and that is a good thing."

Interestingly Debbie Bowman, the captain said, "do you know what I think? If Brian had not felt comfortable, they wouldn't have got on the field."

Michelle Capes recalled the dying seconds of the match. "I remember counting it down and going, 'oh my God', it was almost unbelievable. Like, what the hell? We've just won and oh my God, it was just so crazy."

When the final whistle sounded, the gold medal was Australia's. Not only was it their first ever Olympic hockey gold medal, but the nation's first ever Olympic gold medal in a team sport.

"I don't know what it was like for everyone else, but for me it was a feeling of just massive relief," Sharon Buchanan recalled. "It was almost two years of build-up to that moment, and it was just sheer and utter relief. Then gradually, bit by bit, the joy and happiness started to surface and then thinking of home started to come into your mind. In truth, everything was a bit blank."

Jackie Pereira admitted to similar emotions. "I remember, like most when they are asked their first emotion, it was relief. Because everyone wants you and expects you to win the gold medal as much as you do, and once the siren goes, it is sheer relief because you have done it. Then it's all the other emotions like ecstasy, amazement and joy. I mean, like everyone, we used to sit there watching it on TV never thinking that one day you would end up playing there yourself and winning a gold medal as well!"

They were not alone as Liane Tooth echoed that sense of relief. "When that final whistle went, I think for all of us, we can say the very first reaction was relief."

Loretta Dorman was quoted in *The Canberra Times*. "*When the final whistle went, I had a feeling of relief, after all that hard work there would be no more sandhills, no more guilt. You never realise how much pressure you put on yourself until it's over. It's like releasing a cork from a bottle.*"

"*You wouldn't have believed our team, we were cool. It was a fantastic team, the best bunch I've ever been in. Our captain Debbie Bowman had one of the best tournaments I've seen her play, but it wasn't as though the team needed a leader, we just clicked.*"

"I remember when it finished, I just went, 'thank God that is over'. I remember sinking to my knees going, 'thank God that was over'. It was such a sense of relief," Loretta remembered. "You don't realise how much pressure is built up, built up, built up and you layer it on top and layer on top of layer and you just absorb it, take it with you, absorb it, take it with you, and it was like, 'Wow! Thank God that's finally over.'"

Kim Small, who made way for Lorraine Hillas, remembered leaping off the bench and sprinting onto the pitch when the final whistle sounded. "I can remember running onto the field wanting to be with my 'family' on the field, because you live and breathe in each other's space for four years and you are all focused on the one thing, and when it comes true, it's so special, but also because you have someone to celebrate with. In individual sports, you would have a different scenario. For me to be around 16 other players and your off-field team, I was loving every moment of it and enjoying having the ability to share it with others."

For Elspeth, there were different emotions. "I remember thinking at the final whistle, 'that is the last game I will ever play', which was sad for me, but I was just so happy that those girls had come on, because if they had not received a medal with us, it would have been horrible."

However, Elspeth was not given much time to enjoy the moment. "I was drug-tested. Me and Maree Fish, our numbers came up on the board, and I remember thinking, 'Oh no, I have drunk so much champagne!' Then doc came over and said, 'Did you check the water bottle that you drank from?' I looked at him and went 'nah, you gave it to me, I just drank it.'"

I was in and out quickly, but poor Maree, she couldn't go. You went in and they gave you a sample thing, so Maree and I had to go to the toilet, and they came in and watched you wee."

For Maree, apart from not being able to provide a urine sample, it was a worrying time. "I was sick during the Olympics, and they put me on antibiotics. Then I had to do a drug test after the final, and I was shitting myself. It did take a while and I missed some of the celebrations, I think I may have been with Elspeth. It wasn't very random as it was the two goalkeepers and the two vice-captains. It took a while and took us away from the group and the celebrations. We were in Korea, and had just beaten Korea, so it was very nerve-wracking. I kept thinking, 'What if we lose the gold medal because I test positive for something they gave me when I was ill?' Ben Johnson the sprinter had been disqualified only a few days before and so my heart was racing, as I worried that I would deprive the team of their medal due to medication I had been given. I still have my piece of paper saying I have done the test, but I was thinking, 'Why me?' Particularly because I had been sick and on antibiotics. I think they may even have isolated me for a while."

"Eventually, I gave them what they needed and then I went to the media area, and someone was letting us use the phones, and I was on the phone to Mum and Dad at home."

Maree and Elspeth did make it back in time for the medal ceremony.

In among Australia's joy, there was heartache for the Koreans, the host nation, and for some, it was simply too much. All 16 were crying. Crying "for disgracing our nation". Captain Sang Hyun Chung and goalkeeper Eun Kyung Chung refused to show their faces to President Roh Tae Woo, shaking his hand with one hand and hiding their eyes with the other.

"When we got on the dais and there were mixed emotions, you're there with your teammates but not everyone is there, there were players that were left at home, people that didn't play as much, so there are a lot of mixed emotions in a journey like that," Sharon Buchanan explained.

The coaches do not share the dais with the players but as Peter Freitag recalled, it is still a moment of immense pride. "They got the dais out and we had loads of photos taken and there is one of Brian and I standing in front of the team with our arms around each other, that was just a wonderful moment."

Tracey Belbin also remembered a photograph that was taken at the medal ceremony. "I think we'd had a few swigs of champagne before then, but it was really hot, and I remember we were singing and having a good laugh and just the relief that it was all over and we'd done well, not relief because we felt, 'oh I felt pressure on us to have to achieve something that may or may not come', but just relief because it had been a long time. My interview after it I think was, 'oh, it's so great, all those sandhills at Perth Hockey Stadium were worth it'. I do remember being happy. There's a photo I love and it's very individual of me, but my Mum and Dad were there, and my sisters were there, so they were four people in a crowd of 29,000/30,000 screaming Koreans, and I stepped out of the line when we got our medals and waved to them, and you can see my broken thumb. There's a photo that is shot all the way down the line. So, you can see when I stepped out of the line, but for me that was really a poignant moment that that photo has revealed, because I felt like it was their medal as well because of all the time and money they had invested for me to be there. My parents didn't have a lot of money. But they put in money, time and effort for me to reach that moment. You know, lamington bloody drives and pie drives. People in Mackay that had bought chook raffles every Saturday and helped me, I really appreciated, and still do, all their help to get me to that point. And I love that photo. I love that photo because I know what it meant to me at that time."

"My family didn't travel around the world all the time, but I guess they thought it was an opportunity, and they did everything they could to be there. It was funny because when I broke my thumb, obviously the first that they heard about it was in the news and my Dad said, 'well, I'm not bloody going if she's not playing'. They'd paid all this money and all the rest of it. So, I was so upset. I couldn't speak to them, so I made Loretta ring my Dad and tell him [that] it's going to be okay, they should still come, they think she's going to play. I couldn't talk to him. I was so upset, so emotional, and he was just digging his heels in. 'Oh, she's bloody not going to play, I'm not coming. Not going to fly all the way over there.' So, yeah, it was a funny situation. But they came, and for them it was a massive experience. I didn't really see too much of them. I think, again, it was different to how it is these days. We just trained, and we went back to the Village, and they did their own thing. We saw them after a game for five minutes, maybe. It was pretty rare that you went out and had a day with your family."

Maree revealed that even on the dais with a gold medal around her neck, what they had achieved still hadn't sunk in. "I remember standing on the dais and I had no idea who had given me the medal. I wouldn't have been able to tell you if it was a man, a woman or what. I had no idea until I got home and watched the video!"

"I know that we were all trying to sing the national anthem, but I hate to think what was coming out," she revealed with a laugh. "It was a case of, 'what is this? Oh, it's a medal around my neck, and feel the weight of it. Wow what have we done?'"

With the official ceremony over it was time to celebrate, first with those who had family there, which was not as common at that time, and then together back in the changing rooms.

The champagne did flow but it very nearly didn't. Korean security staff had tried to prevent team manager Yvonne Parsons entering the stadium with it. They failed.

"We cheered and hugged, then we went off the field and people wanted to interview Maree and I," Lorraine recalled. "We just said, 'this is fantastic, eight years of training hard and it's a wonderful result and very exciting to be with such a group of people'. I do remember feeling that was a tad embarrassing, but then thought, 'just get on with it'. Any athlete would find it a tad embarrassing, as you all go to an Olympic Games to play, not to sit on the bench."

"In those days, not many family members travelled to the Games which meant that you relied on each other, and you weren't distracted trying to get people into the Village, or catching up with people, so if there was any down time, we spent it together. I think that helped us pull together as a team."

"My family couldn't afford to be there, and I can't remember a lot of parents there," Sharon Buchanan recalled. "There was not the parental influence we see these days. We did it on our own. That is what you must do, even if you have the support there, at the end of the day you must do it on your own, and I think sometimes today we forget that."

"In this era, very few families could afford to travel to the Olympic Games as airfares were much higher. Even so, in Seoul there were five sets of parents on hand to cheer on the team along with a few fiancés."

Liane Tooth had her family in Seoul and remembered "all our friends and family that happened to be there, they all came down to the track after we had won. Whereas these days that doesn't happen because of security concerns and stuff like that. It was really lovely. My Mum and Dad were there, so to have them come down onto the turf and spend some time with us after we won was really special and also after the medal ceremony."

"I wasn't distracted by my parents being there. They're fairly discreet people and they went off and saw things but, yeah, they were there. I think I saw them maybe once during the course of the Olympics. You could get some passes to bring family into the Village, so on one of the days where we didn't have stuff on, they came in for a few hours and got to show them around and spend a little bit of time with them. I didn't see them much over the course of the Games."

Michelle and Lee Capes' parents were there too, and Michelle recalled how relaxed things were back then to allow them to celebrate with their children. "I remember all of us being down on the athletics track and all the men's players came down and all the Australian officials and Meg Wilson who was the President of the Australian Women's Hockey Association gave my Mum her accreditation, and so she was allowed to come down. She ended up down on the track as well. So that was pretty cool. There is a photo of Lee, Mum and I straight after the match. It was amazing."

As well as very few families travelling to the Olympic Games back then, there were not as many fans travelling as they do today. One fan who had made it to Seoul and via a very circuitous route was Janine Tate from Perth.

"I was 18 years old in 1988 and had spent the year in Japan as a Rotary Exchange student. For the two weeks prior to the Games, my parents came to visit me in Japan to meet my host parents and travel around the country. My parents are sports fanatics, and had attended the 1984 Los Angeles Olympics as spectators, and travelled to Seoul for the 1988 Games after their Japan trip. They had both been involved in track and field in their youth, and my father was an avid hockey player and fan, so these were two of their favourite sports to watch, along with swimming. My Dad went on to attend the 1992, 1996 and 2000 Olympics, it really was his passion. I was not initially intending to go as exchange students are not usually permitted to leave the country during their year of exchange, but my host Rotary Club in Japan had already realised that I was a bit of a sports fanatic myself, and suggested I should go and join my parents. So, I went over to Seoul for the second week of the games," Janine explained.

It was only a 90-minute flight to Seoul but accommodation was a different challenge as Janine revealed. "My parents had flown from Tokyo to Seoul the previous week. Finding accommodation had proved a little tricky, remembering there was no internet and online bookings in 1988! My father was a real estate agent, and he had a South Korean student renting a flat through his business in Perth. He asked the student for advice on which part of Seoul would be a good place to stay for the Games, and the student ended up contacting his family, who invited us to stay with them. So, we stayed in a tiny Seoul apartment along with a Korean family of four, plus their grandfather. Getting tickets before the Games also wasn't as easy as it had been in Los Angeles. Dad had obtained tickets to many of the hockey matches in Seoul through Australian hockey contacts, including Kookaburra Craig Davies. The tickets were very cheap – a ticket to the main part of the stand for the hockey was 3000 won – about AUD\$5.50. We bought most of our Games tickets for other events (swimming, cycling, athletics) from scalpers at the venues. Even with them making a profit, the tickets were still ridiculously cheap compared to Los Angeles."

"This was the first Olympics I had attended, so I was very excited. Given that the tickets were cheap so that the average Korean could afford them, most of the events I attended (swimming, athletics, cycling) had excellent crowds. The hockey crowds were not as big, except when the Korean teams were playing, especially the women's team. There was a lot of security around. As a young Aussie, it was the first time I'd come across guards holding big guns at a sporting event. I think there was a general nervousness about North Korea and the potential for trouble. In general, the South Koreans were extremely welcoming and friendly towards international visitors."

The Seoul Olympic Stadium was set up for the masses. The seating was basic and designed to accommodate as many people in relative comfort as possible. There was however an area where the seating was a little better, and Janine explained how many of the Australians managed to find a way into that area.

"From memory, the hockey venue, Seongnam Stadium, held around 25,000 people. Most of the Stadium seating, I would say around 80-90% was general admission, and these were the tickets that we had purchased for 3000 won. There was a separate, more expensive section that held a few hundred people, and some of the Australian fans, as well as Australian athletes from other sports who came to watch, had tickets to this section. We soon devised a routine to sneak extra Aussies into this section so that we could sit together. Someone from within the 'VIP' section would collect up a few tickets from others seated there, then come outside and pass them to other Aussies so we could enter. In 1988, there were no electronic ticket scanners, so it was relatively easy just to show the tickets and walk straight in. This meant we formed a bit of an Aussie 'cheer squad' in this area of the stand – maybe around 50–100 people for each game. There were other Aussie supporters sitting out in the other section as well, but it's hard to estimate how many. A highlight of the Games for me was sitting next to Dawn Fraser during one of the women's hockey matches. My parents were friends with Sally Carbon's parents and Lee and Michelle Capes' parents, so we often sat with them."

"The women's final was amazing. Playing against South Korea, the Stadium was packed. It felt like about 24,500 cheering for Korea and 500 of us cheering for the Aussies. I remember that we had drawn with Korea in our pool match, so when it was still 0-0 at halftime in the final, I was far from confident that we would get the win, and the crowd was certainly on Korea's side," Janine admitted. Yet come the end of the match, she joined in the celebrations and again gave an insight as to how these were very different times. "When the final whistle blew, we were all jumping around wildly in the stand, and I think there were a few tears from some of the players' family and friends. After the medal ceremony, the crowd cleared out of the venue fairly quickly. Many of the Aussie supporters, including me and my parents, were able to go down onto the pitch and mingle with the players. I remember being so excited to touch one of the gold medals, I think it was Sally Carbon's and I still have my autograph book with all of the players' signatures that I collected straight after the game."

Another Australian who made the journey to Seoul and witnessed this moment of history was Kevin Dempster. "I was 26 at the time and at the peak of my hockey playing career (HWA's Classic League). I went to Seoul mainly to watch and support the Australian men's hockey team. They were the huge favourites to take out the gold, and after so many past disappointments, I really wanted to see them finally win. Public transport in and around Seoul was also quite efficient. The hockey was 20 km away in Seongnam city and was easy to get to by taxi. Taxi fares were quite cheap too. One very clear memory I have is riding an infamous 'Rocket Taxi' from Seoul to Seongnam – these reckless cowboy drivers drove at enormous speed! Getting into the venues, the tight security of the Games came as quite a shock to me despite being warned about it. It was my first time to see soldiers with guns patrolling every street, and to have my bag thoroughly searched at every entry gate."

"I remember almost all of the Aussie women's games that I saw as being very close battles and quite nerve-wracking to watch – against Germany, Korea and Netherlands," Kevin recalled. "But it certainly gave us Aussies in the stand something to really cheer about after the disappointment of the men. The women's final stood out because of the 'surprise' gold of course, and also the very noisy stadium packed full of hometown supporters!"

In 2021, Kevin would be the technical operations manager at the hockey stadium at the delayed Tokyo Olympic Games, where he would witness the Australian men make the gold-medal match, but unfortunately lose in a shoot-out.

Along with the handful of other Australian fans who had travelled to Seoul in the crowd watching the final that day were the Australian men's team, and as Loretta Dorman recalled, they were quick to come and congratulate the women.

"I remember the men coming down and congratulating us. Just milling around the ground and that was just fantastic to have people there that you knew because we'd all really trained together in Perth, on the same field, at different ends. Sometimes we'd play against them, not the complete men's team, but we'd have a muck-up with them. Even a lot of the guys in the Australian team were the ones that were the first intake at the Institute at '84, so we were living together in Noalimba at the time. Some of the girls were going out with them. So, even with the men, it was a very tight unit as well."

"One comment that did come out over our time leading up to Seoul was [that] there was always a lot of focus on the men in Los Angeles, obviously. They were on the *60 Minutes* television show and they were under a lot of pressure to win. I think in Los Angeles we really took on their loss as well, and that definitely affected us in Los Angeles. Basically, we were invested in them winning more than us is how I would put it emotionally."

"That was another one of the things that the team was determined to change, and it was pretty much rightly or wrongly, 'we don't care where the men come'. We train just as much, just as hard, and we basically broke the cycle, and look it's not their fault at all, I think it was just how it evolved over the time and the notoriety that the men's team had got that they were the golden children and I think this '88 team said, 'stuff them, we don't care what they do'. You know what I mean? This is about us, and I think definitely we weren't emotionally invested in their outcome at all, and definitely that has been the case moving forward."

Brian Miller shared a story of how even after the match, that focus and dedication remained in some of the players.

"What we had introduced is commonplace today. Players would come in and score themselves on six or seven different things. That would take two or three minutes. This was self-reflecting, and then we would ask the forwards to tell us what the best things were [that] the backs did today. Then the backs would tell us about the midfield, et cetera. We may also ask them what the best thing was [that] they did in the match. Then we would have a conversation about those observations."

"The previous model had been they would come in from a game – win, lose or draw – and Brian would tell them what he had seen, and Peter may say some stuff, and that was it. When I came in, I said, 'no, no, no, nobody does that anymore. Let's get the input from the kids first.' Of course, some of it is complete and utter nonsense half the time, because the players are caught up in the moment and haven't a clue what is going on, but in other moments, their observations can be pure gold. Sometimes those insights really are gold," Brian explained.

"They were certainly all on a high when they came into the changing rooms [after the gold-medal match], and some had met family outside. They had been kept away from their families, so there were lots of tears and hugging, but not everybody had family there. I went back into the shed, and I suspect I was looking for a beer and there were a handful of players, probably those who didn't have family there, and Kathy was filling in her [evaluation] form. I laughed and took the mickey out of her, but she said, 'no, no I have to do it'. Committed to the very end."

Peter Freitag recalled the aftermath of the match. "We sat at the ground for quite a long time, just having a beer sitting in the changing room, just unwinding. I think the girls were talking about taking souvenirs like some of the flags and then we all thought about Dawn Fraser and the hockey involvement in Tokyo in 1964, and decided it was time to leave. We took the bus back to the Village. Then we had a few more beers and the media came in and I remember stopping drinking and thinking, 'I want to enjoy this night. I want to be able to remember it', and I had a conversation with the two Canadian coaches as I walked to dinner on my own. I was still sober enough, and filled up on food and it was almost a bit of an anticlimax that night because when you have won that gold medal, and you have savoured it, you have achieved what you set out to achieve, it was like... what is next?"

For coach Brian Glencross, who had been deprived of a gold medal in Mexico and had to settle for silver, it was undoubtedly a special moment.

He was reported as saying of the victory: *"What gives me most satisfaction today is that I've developed a particular style in women's hockey and the girls have adapted to it It's entertaining and based on the happy-go-lucky nature of Australians generic play with a lot of flair; I give them the ideas, but they are free to do their own thing, with the accent always on attack."*

He went on to highlight the benefit of having the team together for so long. *"In team sports you have to be together as a team, and I've had eight to 12 girls at the AIS most of the time since the unit began in 1984,"* he said.

"Every game has virtually been a final, especially after the slow start and struggling to draw against Canada early on. Perhaps struggling early was a bonus, but it makes a coach grumpy, but we got better and better. It was tough against Korea in the last round (5-5). Those players in defence had never had five goals scored against them at international level, and I thought we could play better than we did against Holland in the semi-final. That was a crucial game. I made a few minor adjustments to plans, bringing the strikers closer together so as to move the ball better."

While the group has shared the success over the years, Loretta felt that sometimes Brian and his support staff have missed out on receiving the credit that they deserved.

"I think you can't understate the off-field team," she said. "Brian had been on a couple of campaigns. You've got to give credit where it's due. He grew up in an era where it was laughed at that he was coaching women. For example, when he took on the women's job, it was almost like, 'What are you doing that for?' I think the way that he evolved from the '84 campaign to the '88 campaign, just in terms of team management and all of those sorts of things and then to have Brian Miller and Peter Freitag come in, I don't think we can underestimate how that off-field team worked together. They didn't all get on by any stretch of the imagination, but they did professionally. They were in an era where you just didn't let those differences get in the way, you just got on with it. 'We're all going for the common goal'. That attitude absolutely helped and allowed us to do what we needed to do."

6. ONCE THE
MATCH IS OVER

"Where there is unity there is always victory."

Latin writer Publilius Syrus

Not surprisingly once the medal ceremony was over and the team had shared a celebratory drink as a group, the partying began.

As anyone who has played a team sport will tell you, when the partying begins, there is a code of silence – 'what goes on tour stays on tour'.

However, with the passing of time, the team were happy to share some of the things that they got up to following their victory.

As a coach, Peter Freitag allowed the players to let their hair down but he did recall that he and Brian were well aware that "the girls had gone to a toga party with the men's water polo team. They were all handsome, blonde and with muscles, and the girls were wearing togas made from the paper sheets that were on their beds! I didn't go to the toga party, and don't want to know what went on at the toga party, but I am sure they had a good time."

"Oh my gosh, did we party," Elspeth remembered. "We went off with the water polo blokes and then to a Channel Ten party. I remember we weren't great drinkers, so we hadn't had that much but enough for us to be pretty drunk. They were picking us up and throwing us in the air and catching us, and we had absolute faith in them catching us. You look back and think they could have broken our legs or arms, but we were in the moment, those thoughts never even entered our heads."

"They made a pact with us and said, 'Gold medallists aren't allowed to sleep!' The first night I thought, 'that is fine', then the second night, and by the third night I was like, 'we can't do this', so we bolted our door. They climbed up the outside of the building and came through the window and said, 'get up you're not allowed to sleep'. So, off we went again!"

Sally Carbon confirmed that this was the team that didn't sleep. "It was four days, four days and four nights, that we didn't sleep. It's amazing, isn't it, what you can do on adrenalin!"

"There was not a lot of sleep, and the water polo boys were awesome, they had been at all our games, as had the basketballers," Lee Capes recalled. "We had a lot of support from other athletes. We had some good nights."

"The Closing Ceremony was four days later, and Michelle and I share a birthday, and the Closing Ceremony was the day of our birthday, the 3rd of October. We won on the 30th of September, and we had a few good nights in between winning and the Closing Ceremony. It was without doubt a memorable birthday."

Kim Small admitted that the team was lucky that their victory came in the final days of the Games as people were a little more forgiving of their celebrations. "I think we were lucky that our win was at the end of the Olympics, so most of the other sports had finished as well. I think it would have been hard to have that win and be mindful of everyone else still competing after you win a gold medal. There were definitely some late nights, and some very tired and weary bodies on the flight home."

Despite their partying, the girls still managed to fulfil their obligations as Peter Freitag explained. "The next morning, we had to do an interview with Channel Ten and half the girls were still pissed from the night before and they rocked up with no make-up. It was wonderful as we were all over the moon and delighted. We had two or three days of waiting for the Games to end, because the men were playing after us and then a day for the marathon.

So, we had time to enjoy the moment and the medal, and I suppose bask in our success for a bit."

"I felt really pleased for Brian because he was the main driver of it all. He had put his heart and soul into it, and after the Los Angeles disappointment, I think it took a lot for him to bounce back and say, 'Right, we can do this.'"

The one person who is often forgotten is the team manager, Yvonne Parsons. She did a good job, but at the end of it, I am not sure she felt a part of it as she should have."

For Sally Carbon, this was the time when what they had achieved finally sank in. "In the Channel 10 studios when they replayed the highlights, and obviously the production had the overlay of the Australian flag being raised while we were on top of the podium singing the national anthem, that's when all of us went quiet. That was the moment that it hit us. I can still see it. We might have been slightly inebriated at the time too, but that was the moment it dawned on us what we had done, because the game and the crowd was so far away, you didn't get that sense of the moment; also, because you had a Korean crowd who didn't know hockey so well."

"Also, when they raised the flags during the medal presentation, the flags were over the back of the stadium. So, we were all looking around going, 'Where's the flag being raised?' So, yeah, it wasn't until later when you really saw it all jammed together that it really kicked in."

Maree Fish admitted that rather than attending the Channel Ten studios, some of the team would have liked to have kept partying. "We had to come back very early the next morning for some media function which was very disappointing, I don't think any of us got any sleep that night!"

However, the team were happy to go back out to the hockey stadium and watch the men play in their bronze-medal match. "I remember that was hard as we were all feeling very seedy, but you have to celebrate your wins, you work so hard you have to celebrate," Maree explained. "They had supported us, so it was only right that we were there to support them."

Unfortunately, there would not be two medals for Australian hockey in Seoul. The Netherlands claimed bronze with a 2-1 victory. Floris Bovelander scored twice from penalty corners. His first came in the first minute of the match. Australia equalised through Graham Reid just after halftime, but less than a minute later, Bovelander scored again and that was enough to secure the bronze medal.

Looking back on those times, Lorraine Hillas summed up the camaraderie that has stood the test of time perfectly. "We are still partying hard. That's sports people, we all do everything hard. We had a wonderful time."

Returning to Australia, there are still mixed feelings as to whether the team was given the recognition their achievement warranted. Maybe this was because Seoul was the last Olympic Games to be 'amateur'. It may not have been right to celebrate the success so openly.

Yet the Australian medallists had been promised a cash bonus if they were successful and this was the norm. It was a sliding scale with the gold medallists receiving the most.

Despite sending what was at the time the biggest Australian team to an Olympic Games except for Melbourne in 1956 when as hosts, Australia returned from Seoul with 14 medals: three gold, five silver and six bronze.

Swimmer Duncan Armstrong won Australia's first gold medal in the men's 200-metre freestyle. Debbie Flintoff-King won the other gold in the women's 400-metre hurdles.

Maree Fish, who came on late in the gold-medal match, has over the years compared herself to those fellow gold medallists, and quite rightly so.

"I have only played 43 games for Australia but in those games we didn't have interchange. So those 43 games to me are massive, as opposed to some today who have played 200-300 games coming on and off. They were full games for me. Very rarely did I come on at the end. It would have been nice to have played more, but in those days we didn't play a lot. We weren't travelling to the extent that they are now. I am proud of those 43 games, and the most important one was the last one where I only got a minute and 35 seconds!"

"When I used to do talks about Seoul, in my gold medal case I have a bit of paper that tells me the time Debbie Flintoff ran and the time that Duncan Armstrong swam, and I think I am in pretty good company."

For the record, Duncan Armstrong won in a world-record time of 1 minute 47.25 seconds. Debbie Flintoff-King won in an Olympic-record time of 57.17

seconds. So, Maree's time of 1 minute 35 seconds is sandwiched very nicely in between, which completely validates her argument.

While these individual athletes received the bonus from the government for winning gold, the hockey team had to share the amount. as Lee Capes explained. "We heard that the government was giving $8,000 to every gold medallist. Debbie Flintoff-King received $8,000 after winning and Duncan Armstrong received $8,000. We got $8,000 as well, but when divided by 16, it was $500 each, which we thought was awesome, but when you think about it now... there would be hell to pay. We received our $500 and we were rapt. When you don't expect anything, to get things like that was fantastic. That was indicative of our day, we didn't have any financial expectations."

On her return to Australia, Elspeth was quoted in the press. *"As a team it's been disappointing. You think when you win a gold medal little things will happen, but nothing really has. Everyone has really been asking favours and I don't think they realise how much time they demand of all the girls. That's been really hard because every day we're having to do something and it's all just to help them, not us."* She then went on to say, *"If you won an Olympic gold medal in Seoul for Australia you got $8,000, but as a team we had to divide it by 16. I really think something should be done about that. Not many people win gold medals in Australia."*

She went on to say that this was the least that should happen as at that time the athletes had to take time off work to compete at the Olympic Games.

"I think we were one of the first teams to win a gold medal, and I think that caught everyone by surprise," was Maree's Fish's explanation for the money having to be shared before agreeing with Lee Capes. "It was not about the money, it was not about the prestige, we were too early, but I think we set everything up, we set the standard. Now the world has changed, and sport has changed."

Unlike today when all Olympic athletes tend to return to Australia on the same flight, once it was time to go home from Seoul, the Australian women's hockey team split up and went their own separate ways back to their various States.

"We got nothing. You know why? Because they did not expect us to win," Elspeth explained all these years later. "They expected the men to win, but they did not expect the girls to at all. We came back to Perth and there was not a thing planned. Not a thing was done for us, and that was the one thing that upset us. Most of us were from Perth, and yet they did absolutely nothing for us."

"The South Koreans were bloody good, and the incentive for them to win was huge. Even coming second, they received huge rewards as the host nation. I remember thinking, 'I'll be South Korean, thanks.' They received an apartment and a car, they got lots of stuff, and they came second! Imagine what they would have got if they came first."

"It was people outside of hockey who were the ones who did anything for us. They invited us to the grand final of the rugby league [in New South Wales]. Things like that were nice, but it hurt that hockey did nothing."

"I think my memory of it, and over time it's not as clear, but there certainly wasn't a lot organised by way of celebrations" Rechelle Hawkes recalled. "I think it was a bit of a surprise that we won. I remember even the celebrations in Seoul, it was kind of like, 'yeah, that's amazing', but there wasn't a whole lot of fanfare. There was an interview with Channel 10 after the game but we kind of created the atmosphere ourselves. Coming home, there wasn't a whole lot of fanfare to it at all. I mean, looking at the next Olympic campaigns in '92 and '96, then in 2000, the celebration and the atmosphere around any gold medal or indeed, a silver or a bronze, was huge. There was so much fanfare, and there were the ticker-tape parades and everyone around Australia celebrated for months and months on end. But it certainly didn't feel that way for the Seoul gold medal, that's for sure."

Liane Tooth also remembered how understated the reception was on their return. "It certainly wasn't anything like what the Olympic Committee puts on now where they have the welcome-home parades across Australia. The difference between say coming home from Seoul and coming home after Atlanta where the medallists got to do an entire lap of the country was like chalk and cheese. That was a terrific celebration and it was quite different to [the one] after Seoul."

Sally Carbon also agreed that very little was organised once the team returned home, especially in Western Australia. "There wasn't anything organised by Hockey Australia [Australian Women's Hockey Association] or the greater groups, but we had fun. We ended up doing a lot locally but that was independent of the governing body. I do remember the plane journey coming back, because we were in our civvies, we were all told we had to get changed. You can imagine a plane full of Olympians stripping, it was the most amazing experience of athletic humankind that you would ever like to imagine!"

For Lorraine Hillas, some of these local events proved difficult, but looking back she revealed that she learned a great deal from the experience. "When we got back to Perth, we had lots of events to go to, and at times it was hard for me because people would keep asking the same question. Many times, I just wanted to sneak away and not have to answer it again. But that was another lesson. I learnt to put a big smile on my face, take a deep breath and in you go."

For Peter Freitag, arriving home is something he remembers for very different reasons. "When we got back to Perth Airport, my good wife was late, she was nowhere to be seen. She was held up in traffic. So, everyone was being hugged and welcomed home and I was standing there going, 'Is anyone going to hug me?' I have never let her forget that," he said with a laugh.

That understated arrival home in Western Australia was not the case in every State.

"It was fantastic. We flew into Sydney – me and the other girls from New South Wales – and we were met at the airport by our family and friends who all had banners. We knew that the support was there the whole way through the tournament because we were receiving telegrams back then, but to come home and be greeted by the fanfare was a brilliant feeling," Kim Small explained.

"I had spent '85 and '86 in Perth and then moved back to Sydney in '87 and was living with Loretta in Homebush, so we flew back into Sydney as that was our home at that stage. I don't recall if there were any official receptions, but I know club-wise we were definitely recognised. My club Esquires put on a function that night when we got home."

"I then went back out to Tamworth and did an autograph-signing session over a few days. I still try to get back there once a year as there is a tournament out there named after me. So, I do my best to be at that every year and be the face of it and see the young talent coming through."

"The people of Tamworth put on a big event at the Town Hall, and then I did some signings in a shopping centre. It was nice to be recognised, but none of this would have happened if I hadn't started playing in Tamworth. I was given a lifeline to a great career."

Captain Debbie Bowman was one who flew back into Brisbane and found the reception hard to comprehend. "In all honesty, coming home to all the fanfare and the excitement, it didn't feel as if we had achieved what everyone kept patting us on the back for doing. It was all a bit surreal really, and still is today to be honest."

"There were not many events put on from hockey, but from the Gold Coast City Council they did a ticker-tape parade, which obviously being an Olympian and a gold medallist, I was at the front of it. That was special because I sat in the car with my father with a gold medal around my neck, and I can remember thinking, 'Wow this is pretty impressive in your own hometown where you were born and bred.'"

My Dad was so proud, and he is still proud today. He is one Dad that is very proud of my achievements and he often mentions, 'my daughter is an Olympic Gold medallist by the way...' He loves history and sport, so to have his daughter as part of sporting history is a 10 out of 10 for him."

Another to fly into Brisbane was Michelle Capes, even though she was from Western Australia. "I went back to Brisbane because I'd shifted all my stuff, and I was moving to Brisbane with Mark [Hager]. So, I went home with all the Queenslanders and I can't say there were that many people at the airport or anything like that, just family. But they had a ticker-tape parade, and we went to some functions."

"Probably the biggest thing we did is, God knows how, but Parramatta Eels rugby [league] club invited us to one of their big games in Sydney. They put us up at a big hotel, took us to the game. We went out, had big dinners, and then went out with the players and did a lap of honour at halftime. That was unbelievable. It was awesome. We all got given a player's shirt with whoever's number corresponded to our number, and the person who had that number had signed the shirt."

Sharon Buchanan remembered how this all came about and agreed that it was a really special occasion. "Hardie was sponsoring Parramatta rugby league, and they thought that not enough had been done for us, so they flew us to Sydney and we went to all these openings, and they could not do enough for us. It was fantastic and we had a fun time."

"To be honest, it was also quite hard work. You were invited to events, and you had to speak, and then you were invited to schools to talk to the children. For the next 15–20 years, you do a lot and give back a lot as well when you win something like that."

However, as Lee Capes explained, it was very soon a case of 'business as usual'. "I was a 'phys- ed' teacher at the time at Forrestfield High School. Don Knapp, a very famous Australian baseballer was Head of Sport at the time, and when I came back, we had some great celebrations. The night we won, I remember saying, 'This will change my life... and nothing changed.'"

"I did a fair bit of public speaking, I did some speeches with Sam Newman, which meant you had to be on your toes, and Mick Malthouse and a few of the cricketers, which was awesome, and I was also paid, which was good. I then just ended up back in my teaching job."

7. ONCE THE DUST HAD SETTLED

"It is the inspiration of the Olympic Games that drives people not only to compete but to improve, and to bring lasting spiritual and moral benefits to the athlete and inspiration to those lucky enough to witness the athletic dedication."

Australian Olympian Herb Elliott

Eventually, the celebrations died down and the 1988 Olympic Games became a part of history.

Yet this group had made history. They were the first Australian hockey team to win a gold medal at an Olympic Games, in just their second appearance at the Olympics. The men had been competing since 1956 and had carried the weight of expectation but had been losing finalists twice, having to settle for a silver medal in 1968 in Mexico and in 1976 in Montreal.

Some have stated that this was the first team gold medal won by Australia at an Olympic Games. Based on the International Olympic Committee's definition of team sports, this would appear to be correct.

When hosting the 1956 Olympic Games, Australia won three gold medals in relay events. In athletics, they won the women's 4 × 100m relay with a formidable line up of Norma Croker, Betty Cuthbert, Fleur Wenham and Shirley Strickland. They also won two swimming gold medals in relays – the men's 4 × 200m freestyle and the women's 4 × 100m freestyle. Swimming greats Murray Rose and Dawn Fraser being a part of each, respectively.

In Rome in 1960, Lawrence Morgan, Neale Lavis and Bill Roycroft were all a part of Australia's three-day event team that won gold in equestrian.

In 1964 in Tokyo, Australia's sailors won two gold medals in the men's 5½-metre class and the men's star team competition. They also won a gold in 1972 in Munich in the men's dragon team competition.

Then in 1984 in Los Angeles, Australia's cyclists won gold in the men's team pursuit.

While many will argue that these are team events, and the mere fact that some even have 'team' in the competition title, the International Olympic Committee does not view them as team events.

The events that they recognise as team events are as follows: cricket in Paris in 1900, football, water polo, lacrosse in St Louis in 1904, and since then hockey, basketball, handball, volleyball, baseball, softball, beach volleyball, 3x3 basketball and flag football which will appear for the first time at Los Angeles in 2028.

Their definition of a team sport is as follows:

- The entire game or match revolves around team dynamics.

- The outcome depends on collective performance throughout the entire duration of the match.

- The teamwork, strategy and coordination among team members are crucial for success.

- Do not include individual or individual-to-team events within a sport.

When it comes to relay events, these are seen as follows:

- Relay races involve teams, but they are often a series of individual efforts within a team context.

- Each team member runs a segment of the race independently.

- Success depends on both individual speed and the smooth transition between the athletes.

Essentially, the International Olympic Committee characterises team sports based on the impossibility or impracticality of executing the sport as a single-player endeavor, and the entire game or match relying on team dynamics.

Relay races are viewed as events where individual performances contribute to a team's overall success, but they may not be entirely reliant on team dynamics.

So, based on the International Olympic Committee's definition of what is and what isn't a team sport, this group of women also became the first Australian team to win a gold medal since Australia first started competing at Olympic Games in 1896, and since Fanny Durack became the first woman to compete at an Olympic Games for Australia in 1912.

Knowing this, you would expect the team to be held in the highest esteem in Australian sport, yet for some reason they and their achievement have been almost forgotten.

The success of the women's hockey team in 1996 and 2000 has somehow stolen much of the limelight. Why is this so?

Is it because the Olympic Games became professional in 1992 after the 1988 achievement, so there was much more focus on the Games? Was it because the 2000 Olympic Games were once again hosted by Australia in Sydney? Was it because their coach in 1996 and 2000 was the high-profile Ric Charlesworth?

Here is Brian Miller's assessment. "I think it's a bit of misogyny, a case of 'it is only girls'. There was a lovely cartoon in *The Australian* or *The Sydney Morning Herald* the day after the boys lost their bronze-medal match, and they are walking along in the forefront of the cartoon, and the girls are in the background. The boys are saying, 'We played like girls', and then there is one of the girls saying, 'No you didn't!'"

"The coverage at this time [in 1988] was so in favour of men's sport. There was misogyny, there can be no doubt of that. In those days, there were a lot of sports where there weren't even women competing, and in hockey they had only come into the Olympics in 1980, and that was a bit of a pathetic tournament due to the boycott. Then in LA there was only six teams, I believe. Even in Seoul, there were eight teams for the women and 12 for the boys, although these were the best teams in the world. But it was out and out misogyny in my view."

"I think then once the girls won again in '96, they were the Hockeyroos then, and it was all swept up in the excitement of that group, and the original ones were forgotten."

"I think Ric was a part of that. He knew how to work the system, work the media and everything, and I think he was definitely part of that."

"In those days, I think women's hockey was very much a minority sport. Hockey itself was a minority sport. Even in Western Australia where it had great prestige, it never quite had the kudos of other games," Peter Freitag said as he tried to explain the lack of recognition afforded the team.

"It was an amazing achievement. It really was. It may have been overshadowed by the fact that Australia had such a poor Olympics. We only won three gold medals, and everyone was asking, 'What's wrong with Australian sport?' I think that may have detracted from the success of the team. Debbie Flintoff-King and Duncan Armstrong and us, the only gold medallists. If that happened these days, we would be up in arms asking, 'What happened?'"

"It didn't get the recognition it deserved, the media in those days was limited, exposure to the rest of the world was limited, we didn't have social media, there was no Snapchat, Facebook or TikTok, so you were fairly remote and isolated. One TV channel was covering it and the camerawork wasn't very good, the commentary was basic and we did not have any expert analysis. Everything was a bit low key."

"It doesn't detract from the achievement of a gold medal, but I think it did affect the exposure. I don't think that they have been looked up to the way their achievement deserves. Ric Charlesworth's tenure in women's hockey gave them a bigger profile again and much of that was partly due to him because he is a larger-than-life character. Brian was never one to seek the limelight, and that may also have been something."

"Certainly, the girls didn't get the kudos they deserved at the time. When it came to our handling of the media, I am not sure we knew how to do that. I am not sure that those running women's hockey wanted to do that. We had some very pretty girls in this team, which I know sounds sexist, but we all know that if you have a pretty face and are a good athlete, you are a marketable commodity. Perhaps they didn't know how to market the players. There were also some great stories – Elspeth's journey from Kenya to Australia, and others from various backgrounds. Sandy Pisani lost her Dad when young. It was a great mix of personalities and different journeys to Olympic gold."

"The togetherness of this team is also often forgotten. This is what made them great. This was a very together team, and the people liked each other, and this was an important factor."

Rechelle Hawkes was one of the youngest players in the team in Seoul. She would go to four Olympic Games and win three Olympic gold medals. Obviously, each campaign was different, but she shared her view as to why the team from '88 is often forgotten.

"I think because Sydney was the home Olympic Games, that created an incredible atmosphere and a lot of awareness around the Olympic Games, and then the Australian team won that gold medal. I really think that the Hockeyroos' journey from '93 to 2000, we'd built some momentum up, and I think the public really got behind the Hockeyroos and really felt like they were a part of our journey. We had incredible support. I remember in Sydney, the support we had from the general public and the actual viewing ratings on Channel 7 that Olympic Games went through the roof, and our hockey final was one of the largest sporting finals watched by most Australians. I just think the Hockeyroos over that journey created a lot of awareness, and people got right behind the team. I think in '88, because there was that gap in '88 where we didn't win in '92, it was kind of forgotten about. Had we done well in '92, it would've been a different story, and that would've created that momentum, and the success that the '88 team had carved out would have resonated more with the Australian public. I really do think had we performed well in Barcelona, it would've been a different story," she said.

Having been a part of the team for so long and played under both gold-medal winning coaches, Rechelle is ideally placed to compare the two.

"They had some similarities in that they were both old-school. They had high standards. They weren't shy about challenging players. They expected you to meet certain requirements within the team. So that was very similar, but, in terms of their styles, they were very different in their approach."

"Brian was very old-school. He was very much the system that we played, and we stuck with that same system, and I guess the difference between Ric and Brian was Ric brought in some other coaches and they developed different systems of play, and a different game plan. There was just a little bit more variety, I think you would say, a bit more flexibility and variety within the group."

"The disadvantage that Brian had which had a huge impact was not being able to bring a larger squad along the journey, because generally you only played the first 11, so I think it limited the depth that you could start to develop within your squad. When rolling substitutions came in, Ric had that flexibility where he could use the interchange rule to his advantage. So that was a noticeable difference to me, because then you could just bring in so many more players, because you all knew you were going to get a game and share the load. Brian didn't have that where we could share the load as much. So that was a real shift for me, and it changed how you could coach your team."

With three gold medals in her collection, which one does Rechelle cherish the most?

"Sydney for me. It's pretty clear that's going to be the one that I'd cherish the most because it was the last, it was at home and it was a huge Olympic Games."

"The pressure was on. The team was expected to win. We were at unbackable odds, along the lines of Cathy Freeman and Ian Thorpe, so there was that pressure there, that external pressure. It was very special to have family members there too. But Seoul was the start of it, and what I think people do forget is the '88 team paved the way for the Hockeyroos to then continue by being the first team sport to win a gold medal for Australia, and the first Australian hockey team to win a gold medal. That achievement paved the way for the Hockeyroos moving forwards. So, in that sense, it just holds so many dear memories and those players, the ones I started with, I'm still very close to today. So, it's one team that I very much cherish being a part of."

Jackie Pereira would participate in three Olympic Games and would finish with two Olympic gold medals. Looking back, she is pragmatic.

"All I wanted to do was play hockey and I was going to play for as long as I could, and I was fortunate to make three Olympics. I would have loved to have gone to a fourth, but I was getting too old, and I wasn't as quick or as good as I was, so I knew that was never going to happen. I think I stayed on as long as I could, and I am so happy I went to three."

"It was disappointing we didn't do better in Barcelona because we were expected to. You could put that down to pressure, you could put it down to overtraining, you could put that down to things just not going our way. We just scraped into the knockout stage in Seoul, we just missed out in Barcelona. A lot of it is luck. You have to make your own luck, but luck has to be on your side as well."

"I do think that you make your own luck, but you also need things to go your way. We played in Barcelona and we were 1-0 down against Spain, and I think they had never beaten us ever before, but it was in their home country and we did everything to win, we hit the post, we put our stick down for a deflection in front of goal and the ball bobbled before it hit our sticks. Whatever we tried, nothing worked. Then we started yelling at each other and that put us off. Then we became too desperate, so you can 'overtry' as well. If you are in a happy state and things are going well, things will normally happen for you."

"I would possibly say that the Seoul medal means more to me than the other one because it was a bit of a shock, also because obviously Seoul was the first one. We didn't really expect to win it and when we did, it was very much 'deer in the headlights' stuff, we didn't know what to do or what to say. Then in '96 we were expected to win, we played better than every other team there, it would have been a travesty if we had lost. I wasn't playing as much as I probably did when I played in Seoul, and I got injured as well, so that made it harder to get on the field. I was happy that I contributed the same as I had in Seoul, but I am still a team member and still helped in a way, so I am happy about both, but they hold different emotions."

Liane Tooth was another of the team to claim another Olympic gold medal, and she stated that both were extremely special but for very different reasons. "I think they're both on a par, but there's different reasons why. Obviously, Seoul, that was the first team gold medal of any sort, let alone a gold for women's hockey. It was really special to be part of the ones that did it first. But with Atlanta, it was more individually satisfying as well. I feel like I played my best hockey at the Atlanta Olympics, which was obviously before I retired, and we had an outstanding team, different rules, so we played differently. They were both incredibly special, and I couldn't rate one against the other."

As to why the '88 side has been overshadowed by the two other medal-winning sides, she too felt it was where the Australian team was heading into the Games. "At the Atlanta Olympics, we were well and truly established as the world number one and had been for quite a while with Ric at the helm. So, maybe the game was a bit faster and maybe more exciting because of the way the rules had changed. Whether that made the game a bit more dynamic and made it stick in people's minds more, I'm not sure. Maybe the coverage was just a bit different, I'm really not sure."

Sally Carbon revealed that the lack of recognition for the '88 team was not something that she worried about. "The recognition doesn't worry me because I'm very much into being satisfied with myself. It doesn't worry me. It was a different world then. I'm not worried that the '96 and 2000 teams had more recognition. The world was different then. Today we talk about things more, whereas back then you didn't so much. But that was just the era that I went through, '88 and '92. The only thing that's really important is the way we support sport in Australia, which is based on your past performances. So, we've got to perform now! Be it '88, be it 2000, be it the next Olympic Games, to set up our future Hockeyroos going forward, we have to perform because if you don't perform, it's not just bad luck for you, it's not just about you, it's actually about setting things up for the next generation of Hockeyroos. That's really important to me, and this is why I played with so much freedom earlier on. Later on, you actually start thinking about things like this. It's not just a ball, go and run as fast as you can and get it in the net. There's a lot more to it, once you realise the impact of what you're doing."

Whatever the view, there can be no doubting that in 1988 the world was still very much a man's world. Following the success of the women's team, one newspaper headline was: *"Olympic gold tarnished by disaster in men's hockey"*. Even their success was skewed towards the male game.

The opening paragraph of this story hardly gets any better. *"The poor cousins of Australian hockey — the national women's team — finally hijacked the limelight from their star-studded male counterparts in 1988."*

It then went on to state: *"Sadly for the women, the men's demise all but overshadowed their own remarkable achievement."* It is sad to read coverage that was so focused on the men's performance, but unfortunately that was how things were in 1988, even though two-thirds of Australia's gold medals at the Seoul Olympic Games were won by women.

In January 1989, as was the norm in that era, a hypothetical World XI was named. A panel of hockey journalists who attended the Olympic Games was asked to select the best players that year. Six of the Australian team were chosen: Tracey Belbin, Kath Partridge, Jackie Pereira, Sharon Buchanan, Michelle Capes and Lee Capes.

Kath Partridge was also named the world's best goalkeeper for the third consecutive time at a top event.

While many of the team talked about her importance to the side, Sally Carbon explained further. "To me as a young person, the reason why I thought the Hockeyroos could win was because of Kath Partridge. We had a lot of characters in the team, but to me Kath Partridge was a key figure. She was almost unfriendly, but then friendly. She was so driven, but you didn't know it. She could be nasty, but then as soft as a teddy bear. She was just this really interesting character, and from the goals, she was just so strong that she set the tempo, and for a goalkeeper to set the tempo, that was a really unusual formula which I think really added to the success of this team."

The gold-medal match would be Elspeth's last game for Australia as she announced her retirement. Others to announce their retirement were Sandy Pisani and Lorraine Hillas.

Then in February 1989, Debbie Bowman also announced her retirement to return to Queensland to resume her career as a hairdresser, build a home and get married.

Kath Partridge took two years off from international hockey after the 1988 Seoul Olympics. She returned to the team at the Champions Trophy in Berlin in 1991.

The press reported that Bowman, who delayed her marriage to fiancé Rick Sullivan for four years to play in the Olympics, retired for financial reasons. *"After four years with no money, it's time to think about my future. It's time to buckle down and earn some money to put a deposit down on a house. Hairdressing offers the right amount of money but not the time to keep playing hockey. I've sought a 9 to 5 job to help keep me in hockey, but no definite offers have come my way."*

However, her retirement lasted two years, as she explained. "I had two years of retirement, and I wasn't going to play any more internationals, then Daphne Perry who was part of Queensland Hockey asked me to consider going to a State Championships again because we were a little low in personnel, and I said, 'Alright, I'll go.'"

"While I was there, I put up my hand for selection, not thinking I had any chance of going to Barcelona. Hence, I did another two years in Perth, and I had a position change. I went from being a midfielder to a striker, which I thought was a bit unusual for me, and I would say the injuries had started to take their toll. I would always say that I was the fittest in Seoul and nearly as mentally tough as you need to be. In Barcelona I wasn't as fit as I should have been, but I was mentally tough. Had I gone to a third Olympics, I like to think I would by then have had both just right," she said with a laugh.

"Retirement at 25 when you should be almost at your peak as a player was mainly down to money and being able to support yourself and still be able to play and train. A problem that hockey players still face today."

Despite their gold-medal success, Brian Miller explained that it was very hard for the team to cash in on that success. "When we came home after Seoul, it was very evident that people like Duncan Armstrong and Debbie Flintoff-King could make money out of their gold medals because they were in individual sports, and the girls couldn't. They really couldn't. There was nothing forthcoming for them, but of course that is not why they got into it. So, it was alright, as nobody had that expectation."

"Now, not all of the girls have had great lives since that gold medal. They have all had ups and downs in different situations, or health issues and now it's ancient history, it's a long time ago."

"I think as a group they were phenomenally skilful to my naïve eyes. The way they controlled the ball was super. They perhaps weren't as fit as they should have been, but there were some coming to the end of their career who were never going to fit in with all the new fitness regimes, but they were a really good team. Once they beat the Dutch in Perth, I think that they knew they had a chance. The semi-final against the Dutch was probably the best they ever played. It is sad that they have not received as much recognition as they deserve, but I think many of them would say that is OK."

One thing that seems astonishing (but may confirm that no one expected the team to win as many of the team members have said) was the announcement in December 1988, just two months after their gold-medal victory, that the main sponsor of Australian hockey, Esanda, was withdrawing its support.

The company had been involved in supporting hockey since 1979 and had ploughed $1.7 million (roughly $4.4 million today) into the sport. However, it only started supporting the women's game in 1984 and at the time of the announcement only $316,000 (close to $820,000 today) of the $1.7 million had been invested in the women's game.

The reason for the withdrawal of the sponsorship was given by the then Marketing Director Mark Toison, who was quoted as saying: *The basis of the decision, was that Esanda's perceived commercial directions meant a move away from consumer advertising towards concentration on the small business market, which is booming at the moment. Moreover, a market research study over the past 18 months had shown that only 25 per cent of a target audience had been aware of the link between Esanda and hockey.*

Esanda's management denied that the reason that they had withdrawn their support was because of AWHA's public call for sponsorship for the 1990 Women's World Cup to be hosted in Sydney, which had been reported as having offended the company.

Debbie Bowman was asked to comment as captain of the victorious Olympic team and played a very straight bat when she said, "I'm surprised and disappointed at their decision, but thankful for their support, they made the past four years easier for us."

Six months later, there were reports that the men's AIS program was going to be scrapped and scattered across the country. The report stated that *"the move to Perth has been beneficial for women's hockey and that Glencross's charges should stay where they are. It may be ridiculous to separate the men's and the women's, it may not."*

This would be a debate that would rage on every four years from the 1980s up until the present day, usually as the result of Olympic performances. Yet few take the time to look at the structure of the organisation and the way it is operating. Apparently, the location is always the issue. It's funny how the more things change, the more they stay the same.

There can be little doubt that the women's program benefitted from that togetherness with the men's program. Theirs was one of the first such programs in the world. Now that other nations have set up similar programs, the level of competition has become stiffer.

Another reason that the team and its achievement were so quickly forgotten could be the result of comments made to the press by coach Brian Glencross.

As early as 1989, he told the press: *"I think the talent we have got here now is probably better than the talent that came in, in 1985, and that's when we started the program for Seoul. If that's the case, we will be better off, but we must be better by 30 to 40 per cent by 1992 than we were in 1988 if we want to be very competitive in Barcelona. This is not the 1988 team, it's the '89 team with seven new players in it. They have probably had no more than 10 games together internationally and it's going to take time to develop this team."*

Then in August 1991, it was reported that: *"A stern Glencross declared in Perth yesterday the excitement of Australia's success at Seoul was over and with the changes to world hockey, the gold-medal victory would have no significance to the nation's Olympic assault in Spain."*

Glencross said, "The year 1988 has gone and the 1988 team does not exist anymore. Next year's team will be a new team so they cannot possibly be defending Olympic champions. Any talk about us being Olympian (sic) champions may be historic, but it is not relevant to this team. They realise they are going to Barcelona not to win another gold medal but to win 'the gold medal'."

It is hard to tell if those comments played a part in the '88 team being pushed to one side in people's memories, but they can't have helped. While you can understand what he was trying to say, to have the coach of the gold-medal winning side dismiss the achievement in such an offhand way certainly cannot have helped.

The myth is that an Olympic medal, especially a gold medal, will change your life. It will open doors for you. As we have seen, some individual athletes are able to cash in for a short period with advertising contracts which today can set them up for life.

So, has the gold medal changed the lives of this group of women?

"For me 100% it's changed my life," Sharon stated without any hesitation. "I think I am a bit crazy too. I think that sport and life changes you, and I know I am a bit anal about things. I can be emotional about certain things. It does change you I think for sure, but I don't regret it as I feel I had a great experience in the sport."

"Saying that, it wasn't easy. I have had marriage breakdowns, but all those things that the recent players have been through, we have been through that too when things don't work out the way you want them to. I was dropped as captain when Charlie [Ric Charlesworth] came on board, that's just part of it, and I don't regret any of it. I don't even regret losing the captaincy, because those things are what make you who you are."

"I will say one thing about that team. We were a crazy, strong-willed, intelligent group of eclectic hockey players, but we pulled together. We didn't always love each other. Sometimes we didn't like each other and sometimes relationships weren't easy, but when it mattered, we all pulled together. That is something you never forget."

Sharon went on to be captain at the 1992 Olympic Games in Barcelona. Nine players from the 1988 gold-medal winning side were in the squad in Spain. It was interesting to read a comment made by Sharon in the lead-up to the Olympic Games in '92 which shows that even four years on from that first gold medal, it was clear that people had forgotten the achievement.

"I'll never forget that fantastic side we had in 1988," she said. "I feel a bit sorry for some of the players from that team who have retired because everyone is saying that's history now and we have to concentrate on winning here. But it was a great achievement to win in Seoul."

Maree was another who felt that it had impacted her life. "I think I would have to say, 'yes it has', but it's not just the medal. It is what I have done after that as well, and what that has allowed me to do."

"It certainly didn't open doors. I think at the time that we won, the world wasn't ready, or maybe Australia wasn't ready. I am not sure the right answer to that. Tasmania perhaps wasn't ready, or maybe I wasn't ready for it. Perhaps I didn't want to be public property, that is probably more likely."

"I know in '91 when I was dropped from the team, my world fell apart, and it was not until a little bit further down the track when I did my honours thesis all about retirement from sport, and that proved to be my counselling, my catharsis for moving on. I interviewed people about how their sporting career ended, injury, retirement, [and] being dropped against retirement of your own choice. Injury, retirement and being dropped being the worst. I should have probably pursued that more in my studies, at one stage I was going to do a PhD. But I didn't do that, and life took another turn."

"Hockey has been such a keen part of me developing as a person. From that thesis I became involved in retirement from sport, and then a friend of mine from Western Australia had won a scholarship to go to England and study through Rotary, and she put me onto Rotary and I won a scholarship that funded me to go to America for a year and I studied athletic counselling. There was a lady from the VIS (Victorian Institute of Sport), Deidre Anderson, and she did a lot of career education at the AIS, and I had studied under some of the gurus in this field in America at Springfield College and I did part of a master's there. From this specific athletic counselling course, I went back to Tasmania and got a job as the Athlete and Career Co-ordinator at the TIS (Tasmanian Institute of Sport)."

"All of that, the hockey, the gold medal, falling down after the gold medal, trying to get to Barcelona, and then picking myself up off the floor and dealing with that led to all these other things." Maree paused before adding, "Looking back, Barcelona made the lustre greater."

There was another long pause before she said, "I reckon it has, it is a pretty special bit of metal!"

For Lorraine, who like Maree faced the frustration of not getting on the pitch until the dying minutes of the gold-medal match, there is also understandable pride in being part of such a special group.

"I am just ever so privileged and grateful," she said. "To play for your country and to hold a medal as you get older, and for that medal to be gold, it gets more special as the years go by. When I look at my daughter Georgia, I think, 'wow, some of these kids today are so good and they never get that opportunity'. So, it makes me realise how lucky am I that someone when I was 18 said, 'Let's pick her.'"

"I played for Brisbane, Queensland and then made the Australian squad all in the same year, and I never went looking for it. So, to look back, Brian picked me and he gave me this opportunity to have this part of my life that is so significant, and that helped define the person I became. It gave me these fabulous friendships that have lasted a lifetime. I wouldn't ever knock that back."

"Those friendships, the camaraderie, and the sense of sisterhood is something that needs to be recorded. None of us were jealous or down on each other. I don't know how it happened, I am not sure if possibly Brian Miller helped with that, but we always got on well, laughed and had fun, and we still do."

Even looking back at the game time she received in Seoul, Lorraine has been able to turn that experience into a positive. It is a measure of her as a person.

"It was not the ideal situation for someone who has been to two Olympics, but I think if you put yourself out there, you have to accept what people choose for you. Did it change my life? Did it define who I am? No, but it did define how I see the world, and hopefully how I treat others. With everything there is a learning experience, and so for me in my teaching and when I coached, I go out of my way to make sure that everything is equal, and everyone is treated fairly. To be honest, sometimes I probably get it wrong, but my intent is to treat people fairly. I learned that from the situation I was put in, and I am really grateful for that. When I look back, was it what I wanted? No, but did I learn more about life? Yeah, I did, and I hope it has helped me as a person and a teacher and when I coach kids. However, in no other way has it changed my life. That medal hasn't set me up for life."

Rechelle had a different take on whether her medal, or medals, had changed her life. She admitted that in some ways it had, but when it all came down to it, even Olympic gold medallists face the same issues as everyone else in life.

"I think it changes your life in that you're a very small cohort of people in the world that has an Olympic gold medal. There's not many, I think it's – I'm not sure of the exact number – but it's 1% or less people in the world that have an Olympic gold medal. So, you're in really rare company, and it's something that the average punter just looks at it and goes, 'wow, I would love to have one of those'. That, for me, is where it has changed my life. In that you're in very rare company, not many people have an Olympic gold medal, and when you meet other Olympic gold medallists, you can kind of just nod and say, 'yeah, we did it'. So that, for me, is where it has changed my life, and then when you settle down and you have a family and get on with the business of life, you're just like everyone else that lives through the same sort of day-to-day issues and trials and tribulations. So, yeah, the answer to that question whether it has changed my life is yes and no. It certainly does change your life, but then in other ways it's just business as usual and you just get on with your life like everyone else."

For Sally, the thing she has found challenging is that despite all that she has achieved since winning the gold medal, it is the overriding thing in her life that most people remember her for.

"There's always good and bad with things like this. I can't walk into a meeting, I can't do anything, meet someone or anything, without someone saying, 'oh, she's an Olympic gold medallist'. This is 30-plus years later. Still to this day that's your brand, and that's also not a good thing."

"When you think about it, in my case I won that gold medal at 21 but I'm now in my 50s. Over 30 years later, despite a hell of a lot of work, I'm known for something that I did at 21. People don't think that you've got three degrees, that you're chairing this, you're doing that, or you've contributed to society here, there and everywhere. All everyone thinks about is you at 21. So, there is good and bad in it, but, of course, I'd never give it back. It's not the gold medal that is the most important thing to me. It's the fact that this group of girls did something absolutely ridiculous together. We climbed a mountain together, and succeeded together, and that's what the gold medal represents. It doesn't represent a hockey tournament, it represents that togetherness, that unity."

Like Sally, Tracey revealed she was determined that the gold medal was not going to define her life. Yet in terms of whether it has changed her life, she too felt that in some ways it had, and yet it hadn't in others.

"It's a really hard one because for some people I think it defines them, and I tried to not make it do that. I went on and studied and did a different range of things. I never thought I'd coach. I never thought that I would coach after I played. I thought, 'how boring, what a boring job', and then I got into it and I travelled to South Africa and America and coached nationally here in Australia and with the juniors. So, I think, 'yes it has'. I wouldn't say it has opened doors. I don't think I've got on the bandwagon, and I'm not involved like some people are because of their status due to their achievements. But I wouldn't have had a life where I can go to a dinner and meet other athletes or get called out to an Olympic slide event and mix with other medallists and meet kids. I wouldn't have had that aspect in my life, and while those opportunities are thinning out, I still get – as my sisters say – I get 'rolled out' every four years and that's terrific. That recognition is really nice, and I'm quite happy to share my experiences with people. So, having that in your life I think adds to your life. I wouldn't say it's changed my life, but certainly added to my life."

"I was always going to play hockey. I always liked hockey. Now I'm back involved at a local level with hockey, and I like it. If you're coaching, I will say that because you've been there, you've done it, you've experienced all the highs and lows, you know it. I've experienced selection, non-selection, injury at the Olympics, all the things that go with that. Being at the Institute, leaving the Institute and having to do stuff on my own, so I have a lifetime of experiences."

"There are other lives. You live this much bigger part of your life outside of that, half the people you meet don't know that part of your life and that's okay.

You just want them to accept you how you are. I think people forget that you are a normal person. Every Olympics, the medal comes out. People ask me where I have it, and my Mum used to look after it because until I came back and lived in Mackay near my parents, she kept it for me. They used to ask, 'Where is it?', and I would say, 'well, it's in my Mum's undie drawer probably, I don't know'. Around the Olympics every four years you get it out, I wouldn't really any other time."

"I guess I just wanted to do the best I could when I was given the opportunity, and so I didn't expect it to open doors for jobs. That's when I used to get a bit annoyed, when you have athletes, not necessarily hockey, but athletes that hadn't stayed or didn't have the qualifications, but they expected to be the CEO of a company. With what? I used to ask why would they go to that company if they've hired that guy? What do they have to offer? Winning a gold medal doesn't make you good at running a company!"

"So, I would say it has given me opportunities that I wouldn't have had, but it hasn't really changed my life."

Loretta had a very similar opinion to both Rechelle and Tracey in terms of what the medal has given her and whether it has altered her life.

"It's an interesting thing from my perspective because whilst I've won a gold medal for my country and for my team and stuff like that, personally I don't know whether I played the best I could've ever played in that tournament, introspectively," she revealed. "I think that's just how I feel when you look at your game and you go, 'Well I won, but how well did I play?' I think you realise what you've done when you see how happy other people are. I think that's when it really resonates, when you come home and you have a photo with your family and it gets in the papers, and you're invited into the Olympian's Club, and you go to an Olympic celebration and you go up on stage. Those sorts of things make you go. 'wow, this is pretty big'. I think that's probably the biggest acknowledgement for me to be a part of the Olympian's Club. The realisation that you're part of such an elite group. I definitely think that makes it a big, big difference."

"I don't think the medal can actually change your life, because regardless of what you want, you've got that and then we got the OAM [Order of Australia

Medal] as well, so you've got that acknowledgement from your government. That definitely, absolutely, puts a smile on your face. Does it change your life? Does it open doors? I don't know whether it would, it probably does open doors if you want to use it to that effect. It definitely gives you a lot of self-esteem, absolutely. You feel quite confident in your own skin, a little bit more than you might have."

"It definitely gives you a place within your sport, as it's something that people aspire to. I coach a lot of 15-year-olds and younger kids now, and it's always lovely to take the medal out and they're just going, 'Oh wow, I want to get one of those.' So, does it change your life? Yeah, absolutely it changes your life because you can do things with it and you can go to schools. You are able to impact other people's lives. I loved going to schools and, thanks to the medal, can encourage young people in the sport, or even those not in the sport. I think that's how it changes your life, the people you get to meet. In that way it absolutely changes your life."

According to Jackie, with the passing of time the memories are beginning to fade, but some people still remember. However, like Loretta, she enjoys encouraging the children, the next generation, by sharing her memories of that time.

"It has changed my life a little bit but not greatly. It's great that sometimes every four years we get the recognition that we deserve, but the more years that go by, no one really remembers. Sometimes I can go to the shops and say my surname and they will say, 'Do you know the girl that played hockey?' or something to that effect and I will say, 'well, that's me'. So, the name gets remembered every now and then," she said with a laugh.

"I work at a school, so every four years I bring out all my uniforms and gold medals and give talks around the school leading into the Olympics. The kids get a little enthusiastic about those Games and interested in the Olympics, which is great."

"One thing that I think is good [about] being a hockey player is if you were a swimmer or a runner you probably would not be able to walk down the street without being recognized. At least we have that anonymity and what we achieved is only noted if people recognise us, so I guess we get the best of both worlds," she said with another laugh.

Elspeth shared the view of many of her teammates when she said without any hesitation that realistically, winning the gold medal had made little difference to her life. "It's great to have it, and when you go places and you are introduced as a gold medallist that is nice, and that you have an OAM, but it doesn't make any difference to your life, not like a swimmer where you get massive endorsements. It's not really made any difference."

"No, no, not at all. Not at all. I wouldn't half the time even remember I've got it," was Michelle's response. She admitted that she found it hard always to be known or introduced as an Olympic gold medallist. "Yes, it annoys the crap out of me. They go, 'oh my God, she's an Olympic gold medallist', and I go 'oh, I just don't have it planted across my forehead'. It has an impact on your life, but it doesn't change it."

Having had Mark Hager as her boyfriend at that time and subsequently marrying him, the question that had to be asked was how hard was it when the men came fourth and the women won gold in Seoul with them being a part of those respective teams.

"Oh, don't you worry, I don't need to remind Mark because everybody else does!" She said it with a laugh before admitting, "I felt a little bit torn because I wanted to really celebrate, yet I didn't want to do it in front of him."

Mark went on to win a bronze medal in Atlanta in 1996.

Kim Small was sure that it hadn't changed anyone's life dramatically, but once again highlighted how the group has managed to remain friends all these years. "No, I don't think so, what it has done is give us a lifetime of friendship with some special people and it's always nice to be able to give back to the sport when you can. But I don't think it has changed any of our lives. It probably gave some of us some direction where we went with our lives as in coaching or marketing, those types of things, but that is all."

Captain Debbie Bowman-Sullivan agreed. "No, not at all, not at all. Nothing changed at all. I think that this is again a reflection of us as a team. I don't think anyone has pushed themselves forward or highlighted that they are or have been treated as any more special than the rest, and I think that has been a good thing. Everyone has just gone about doing what they would do normally. Most important of all, we are all still friends and able to laugh together whenever we catch up."

On 12 February 1989, the ABC's Managing Director David Hill announced the recipients of the ABC Sports Awards for 1988 at the Melbourne Hilton.

Two awards were presented – one for the most outstanding athlete of 1988 and the other for the most outstanding team of the past year.

Debbie Flintoff-King received the individual award for her contributions to the world of track and field and her gold medal-winning performance at the Seoul Olympics. The team award went to the Australian women's hockey team for their efforts in winning an Olympic gold medal in Seoul.

Among the other team nominees were the Australian women's Test cricket team, the VFL premiership team Hawthorn (the AFL had not started by then) and the Australian men's soccer team, the Socceroos.

At a later event in Sydney, Debbie Flintoff-King won her second Australian Sportswoman of the Year Award. This time, the Victorian track star won the award ahead of a distinguished field that included fellow Olympic medallists Loretta Dorman and Elspeth Denning (hockey) and Lisa Martin (marathon).

Many of the gold-medal winning hockey players from Seoul also received honours in their individual States, such as Loretta Dorman who at the 1988 Capital Television ACT Sports Star of the Year Awards, won the overall Sports Star of the Year Award as well as the Female Sports Star Award.

In Western Australia, Elspeth made a clean sweep of that State's awards, winning the Caltex Sports Star of the Year Award, Sportswoman of the Year and the Lindy Award.

The last award is one that many may be unfamiliar with. It was created back in the 1950s and was very prestigious. The Sportsmen's Association of Australia was established in the 1950s "to foster interest in sport and mobilise support for charities". The presentation of the Lindy Award, which was named after the Association's founder, Walter Lindrum, was an annual event. Initially, the Association compiled lists of the best 'sportsmen' of the year by polling sports magazine and newspaper editors throughout Australia. Despite the use of the phrase 'sportsmen', the Award was open to and, at times, won by women.

It is interesting to note that as the Association's structure evolved, so did the format of the Lindy Awards, shifting in the early 1960s to State finalists for the Lindy Award running for Australian Sportsman of the Year. Note that the name was not changed to 'Sportsperson'! That was another sign of the times that carried over into the 1980s. Only in 1995 did it change to State Sportsperson of the Year when Queensland led the way.

Every member of the 1988 gold medal-winning team has been inducted into their State Hockey Association's Hall of Fame over time. The team itself was inducted into the Sport Australia Hall of Fame in 2003, and some of the players have also been inducted individually into the Sport Australia Hall of Fame.

However, only seven players and coach Brian Glencross are in the Hockey Australia Hall of Fame.

Several sporting stars have uttered the words, "Trophies gather dust, memories last forever." Never were those words truer than with this remarkable group of individuals. Individuals from different backgrounds, different places in Australia, and with very different personalities who saw the best in each other, put aside their differences to achieve a shared goal.

As several have said, they can walk down the street, and no one knows they were part of Australia's first-ever team to win a gold medal at the Olympic games, let alone the first-ever hockey gold medal. Some may like that anonymity, and that is understandable.

Yet whether they like it or not, on 30 September 1988 at the Seongnam Stadium in Seoul, they all wrote their names into the history books with that 2-0 victory over the hosts, South Korea. That was their moment, and long may it live with them.

For the rest of us, we must never forget their achievement and continue to use their success to inspire others.

AFTERWORD

The reason for writing this book was to record an important part of not only Australian hockey history, but also Australian Olympic history.

My goal was to capture the individual stories of those involved in this special moment before they and their personal memories were gone forever.

Unfortunately, no sooner did I start work on the project than Kath Partridge passed away. Then came the shock to all, as none of her teammates even knew she was sick, when Sandy Pisani passed away.

I was unable to speak to either.

To try and ensure that their stories have been included, I have spoken to friends and family who have shared information with me. I have also searched archive newspapers for comments and stories that may give us an insight into their thinking at the time.

A special thanks to Jane Lamprey, Susie Watkins, Warren Murphy and Greg Partridge.

We have also lost team doctor Tony Galvin and coach Brian Glencross. I was fortunate to talk to Brian when I wrote *Australia's Hockey Grail,* and Brian Miller kindly asked Brian questions about this book when he visited him during his illness. I was never able to speak to 'the doc', although according to everyone, he would have probably told me what he always told them – "take a Panadol and lie down".

Just because they are no longer with us, they should never be forgotten, for they, too, were an essential part of this piece of Australian sporting history.

Ashley Morrison

The future belongs to those who believe
in the beauty of their dreams.

Eleanor Roosevelt

More really good books from Fair Play Publishing

Turning the Tide
by Michelle Ford-Eriksson

George Best Down Under
by George Best

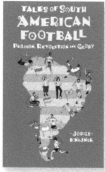

Tales of South American Football – Passion, Revolution and Glory
by Jorge Knijnik

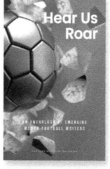

Hear Us Roar – an anthology of emerging women football writers
Compiled by Bonita Mersiades

Noddy – the Untold Story of Adrian Alston
by Adrian Alston

Encyclopedia of Matildas
by Andrew Howe

The First Matildas – the 1975 Asian Ladies Championship
by Dr Greg Downes

Available from fairplaypublishing.com.au and all good bookstores

FAIRPLAY
PUBLISHING

Milton Keynes UK
Ingram Content Group UK Ltd.
UKHW050020010724
444821UK00006B/15